TOP **10**
MARRAKECH

CONTENTS

4

Introducing Marrakech

18

Top 10 Highlights

MARRAKECH

INTRODUCING

A riad in Marrakech

WELCOME TO
MARRAKECH

Few cities can rival the dynamic cultural tapestry of Marrakech. Here, you can marvel at Islamic architecture, admire fine French gardens and shop for global crafts in the souks – all in one day. Don't want to miss a thing? With Top 10 Marrakech, you'll enjoy the best the city has to offer.

Located in the foothills of the Atlas Mountains in the northwest of Africa, Marrakech has long been a cross-roads of civilizations, and the city's African, European and Middle Eastern cultures are deeply intertwined. A stroll through the cobblestoned alleys of the ancient Medina reveals these eclectic influences, with covered spice and textile markets testament to Marrakech's role as a centre of global trade. The beauty and intricacy of Islamic design is on shimmering display, from the towering minaret of the Koutoubia Mosque to the

Local life at the Medina

Saadian grandeur of Ben Youssef Medersa. At the heart of it all is the endearing chaos of the central square, Jemaa el-Fna, where street performers and traditional musicians entertain passersby, and food vendors serve abundant, aromatic dishes. And if the urban bustle gets too much, Marrakech's *hammam* bath houses offer pampering of the highest order. With a host of splendid gardens to unwind in, including the famous Jardins Majorelle, there's no denying the sensory allure of the Red City.

And this is all without venturing beyond the ochre walls of the Medina. Outside the ancient centre, you'll find the Saadian Tombs necropolis in the Kasbah and the dizzyingly ornate Bahia Palace in the Mellah, the city's former Jewish quarter. It might be rooted in tradition, but Marrakech is also defiantly modern: the New City districts of Guéliz and Hivernage offer shopping boutiques, design hotels, lively nightlife and innovative contemporary dining.

So, where to start? With Top 10 Marrakech, of course. This pocket-sized guide gets to the heart of the city with simple lists of 10, expert local knowledge and comprehensive maps, helping you turn an ordinary trip into an extraordinary one.

THE STORY OF
MARRAKECH

When Amazigh farmers built a small settlement close to the Tensift River around 10,000 years ago, they could never have foreseen the role their village would play in global history. It has since weathered warring royals, Ottoman invaders and European colonizers, before becoming the city it is today. Here's the story of how it came to be.

Laying the Foundations

The site around what is now Marrakech was initially settled by Neolithic agriculturalists. It wasn't until the early 11th century that the Almoravids, a native Amazigh dynasty, established the settlement as their new capital, choosing the site due to its position at the intersection of Saharan trade routes. Thanks to favourable trading relationships and the coalition of nomadic peoples throughout what is now Mauritania and the Western Sahara, the Almoravid empire soon spread across two continents, incorporating southern Spain and parts of sub-Saharan Africa. The stage was set for the city's unique tapestry of early architectural styles. The Almoravids constructed the city's earthy red ramparts to enclose the Medina using a mud-and-lime mixture. The empire was also responsible for creating the city's irrigation system, which sources water from the Atlas Mountains and filters it through a network of underground channels, known as *khettaras*.

The Almoravids lost control of Marrakech to the ambitious Almohad dynasty in 1147, and it was under these new rulers that some of the city's finest monuments were created, including the Koutoubia Mosque. Though the city saw some great achievements throughout the 12th century, Marrakech was riven by a succession of tribal feuds and

Almoravid Koubba, erected by the Almoravid dynasty

slowly fell into a state of decline,
until the capital was moved to Fés.

Shifting Fortunes

Marrakech regained its capital status
in the early 16th century under the
Saadian dynasty. The dynasty would
help the city navigate Ottoman
invaders while restoring Marrakech
to its former glory. Saadian sultans
amassed vast wealth, constructing
well-known treasures such as Ben
Youssef Medersa and the palaces and
gardens of Mouassine.

This Saadian glory was short-lived,
however, as the ascendant Alaouite
dynasty captured the city in 1669.
Echoing events of the 12th century,
the Alaouites again moved the capital
to Fés, and Marrakech was to fall into
disrepair once more.

The city faded into obscurity
until Mohammad III of the 'Alawī
dynasty restored it to capital status
in the mid-18th century. His reign
as Sultan would set in motion over
a century of peace.

**Moulay Abd al-Rahman,
Sultan of the 'Alawi dynasty**

Moments in History

1062
Almoravid dynasty founds
Marrakech as its capital, establishing
control of a major hub on the
Saharan trade route.

1147
The Almoravids lose control of
Marrakech to the Almohad dynasty.

1549
Saadians overthrow the Merenids
becoming the first Arab dynasty
to rule Morocco.

1668
The Alaouite dynasty sweeps aside
the Saadians, and continues to rule
today under King Mohammed VI.

1750
Mohammad III of the 'Alawī
dynasty restores Marrakech to
capital status and presides over
a period of peace in the city.

1912
Treaty of Fés makes Morocco a French protectorate and Resident-General Hubert Lyautery enlists Henri Prost to design Guéliz, the new city of Marrakech.

1918
Amazigh tribal leader Pacha Thami el-Glaoui is enlisted to rule over Marrakech and southern Morocco.

1947
French painter Jacques Majorelle opens his private gardens Jardin Majorelle in Guéliz to the public.

1955
Mohamed V is crowned king; a year later Morocco declares independence from French rule.

2023
An earthquake measuring 6.8 on the richter scale claims around 3,000 lives in Marrakech and the neighbouring Atlas Mountains.

French Protectorate

The city's peace came to a turbulent end at the start of the 20th century. The French military occupation of Morocco began with the invasion of Oujda and the bombardment of Casablanca in 1907. This display of might led to Sultan Abd al-Hafid signing the Treaty of Fés in 1912; so began the French protectorate.

Under French control, European architecture, culture and education systems were implemented in Marrakech. In order to preserve the integrity of the city's ancient Medina, Resident-General Hubert Lyautery initiated the construction of a new town, Ville Nouvelle. It became known as Guéliz, an offshoot from the French word for church, *église*. The town was designed by French planner Henri Prost, with wide Parisian-style boulevards, walled gardens, Art Deco apartment blocks, villas, and grand 1920s-style theatres, cafés and cinemas. During the mid-20th century, many French artists, including Jacques Majorelle, made their home in Guéliz.

Alongside French governance, Marrakech was administered by a local

French generals arrive in the city in an armoured car, 1912

Enjoying the view from a terrace in the UNESCO-listed Medina

"Pasha", or administrator. Thami el-Glaoui, an Amazigh ruler known as the "Lord of the Atlas", served as Pasha until 1956; he was sympathetic to the French protectorate, charming many global leaders and accruing huge wealth during his time in office.

Post-independence Boom

But all was not well in French Morocco. Rising tensions at French governance led to the formation of the Moroccan National Front, and in 1952 and 1953 several anti-French demonstrations were repressed with bloodshed. The rising disdain for French rule led to Morocco gaining independence in 1956, after the signing of a declaration in Paris to replace the Treaty of Fés and to reinstate the sultan.

Post-independence, the city expanded rapidly to the west, with a new modern downtown connecting the Medina with the affluent neighbourhood of Guéliz. The years that followed brought swathes of visitors to Marrakech, from alternative travellers attracted by its spiritual landscape and cheap living, to fashion designers, movie stars and music legends, including The Beatles and Rolling Stones. Later, they were joined by tourists: numbers in the capital were to double between 1965 and 1970. Fast behind them were foreign investors, who swiftly arrived to renovate former palaces into luxury homes and riad hotels. As tourism boomed, the United Nations stepped in and declared the Medina a UNESCO World Heritage Site in 1985.

Marrakech Today

International interest and investment continues with tourist numbers on the rise again after a brief COVID-19-related hiatus. Confidence in the city as a global destination is reflected in the opening of new five-star international hotels offering the height of luxury.

This largely rosy picture was shattered by the catastrophic earthquake that shook the city and claimed 3,000 lives in 2023. Many popular tourist sites were closed for repairs for several months, but by mid-2024 many had reopened. Due to a strong sense of collective optimism, Marrakech's future looks bright, with a plethora of new developments and a headline-grabbing spot hosting the 2030 FIFA World Cup.

TOP 10
EXPERIENCES

Planning the perfect trip to Marrakech? Whether you're visiting for the first time or making a return trip, there are some things you simply shouldn't miss. To make the most of your time – and to enjoy the very best this wonderfully varied city has to offer – be sure to add these experiences to your list.

1 Get lost in the Medina

Entering the labyrinthine alleys of Marrakech's ancient Medina is a unique form of time travel. Within this dense warren of streets – where vendors hawk wares amid the aroma of rich spices – getting lost is actively encouraged. So forget your planned route and soak up the endearing chaos.

2 Unwind in a riad

Once the exclusive homes of the city's wealthiest, many of Marrakech's traditional riads (p114) have been converted into luxurious guest houses. Few lodgings offer tranquillity like this: thick walls block out the bustle of the nearby souks, while courtyard gardens offer a cool space in which to relax.

3 Make for a museum

With such a storied history, it's no wonder Marrakech does museums so well. The city's past is on display at a range of exhibitions: learn about the Indigenous Amazigh at the Pierre Bergé Museum of Berber Arts (p39) or marvel at the intricacy of Moroccan art at the Dar el Bacha Museum (p45).

4 Admire incredible architecture

Waves of settlers have contributed to the city's architectural medley. Gems include the Koutoubia Mosque (p28) with its soaring 12th-century minaret, a (literal) highpoint of Amazigh design. Ben Youssef Medersa's (p34) scripted walls and zellige tiles are a must-see.

5 Ponder contemporary art

The city is fast evolving into a hub of modern art thanks to a new wave of contemporary galleries. To see all the dazzling new faces of Moroccan art and graffiti hit the David Bloch Gallery (p46) or visit MACMA (p46) to see the work of artists like Jacques Majorelle.

6 Try traditional tangia

Referring to both the clay pot and the slow-cooked meat within it, *tangia* is synonymous with Marrakech. The pot rests on embers for hours, resulting in a melt-in-your-mouth stew. Visit Jemaa el-Fna (p22) to see stalls serving it up just as they have for centuries.

7 Go shopping in the souks

This is perhaps the definitive Marrakech experience. Wandering the souks (p26) can be as bewildering as it is thrilling, the bustling lanes full of stalls selling carpets, spices, kaftans, jewellery and plenty more. Come ready to bargain: a world of treasures awaits.

8 Relax in a hammam

Navigating Marrakech can be an exercise in endurance. Luckily, the city offers a perfect solution: the venerated ritual of the *hammam*. The hot steam rooms and exfoliating scrubs at spots like Les Bains de Marrakech (p48) are designed to leave you feeling restored.

9 Have a night out in Guéliz

The modern, affluent area of Guéliz bursts into life at sundown, with international chefs plying dishes at hip restaurants and top DJs drawing crowds. Our suggestion? Start with cocktails at Barometre (p59) before dancing on the So Lounge terraces (p90).

10 Escape into a green oasis

The city's beautifully manicured gardens and greens perfectly offset the bustle of the Medina. The ornate water features and tree-lined avenues of havens like Le Jardin Secret (p50), and Anima Garden (p51) provide a shady oasis when things get too hot.

ITINERARIES

Seeing the Koutoubia Mosque, strolling the Jardins Majorelle and shopping the souks: there's a lot to see and do in Marrakech. With places to eat, drink or take in the view, these itineraries offer ways to spend 2 days and 4 days in the Red City.

2 DAYS

Day 1

Morning

Spend your first morning getting to know the ancient Medina. Starting at Bab Doukkala, head across the square. Thronging with vendors, it's a taste of what's to come in the nearby souks (p26), where narrow streets are lined with shops and artisans – you could lose a whole morning exploring this dense warren. When you're ready, stroll along rue Sidi Abdelaziz, a shopping area home to fashion boutiques, art galleries and *hammam* spas. Continue past the Royal Palace, the king's official residence, and turn onto rue du Mouassine. This neighbourhood dates back to the Saadian dynasty, before many wealthy aristocrats built their

DRINK
With a healthy menu, large social space and a bike rental business, Pihala Café (p79) in the Medina prides itself on being a communal hub.

grand residences here in the 16th century. It's now time to head to Le Jardin Secret (p50), a beautiful palace set in a garden oasis. Just across from the gardens is Café Arabe (p79) with a seasonal Moroccan-Italian menu.

Afternoon

Refreshed, head east to Ben Youssef Medersa (p34). Built by a Saadian sultan, it was once the largest Islamic college in the country and is a marvel of Islamic architecture. Afterwards, walk south through the labyrinthine streets to visit Jemaa el-Fna (p22), Marrakech's main square. There's no centre quite like it: smell the fresh orange juice, marvel at the peddlers of traditional medicines and listen to the lively yarns of Amazigh storytellers. Wonder gives way to wonder: the Koutoubia Mosque (p28) lies just around the corner. Non-Muslims can't enter the mosque, but can marvel at its towering minaret and listen to the resounding call to prayer. This evening head for dinner (and a dance, if you're partial) at Comptoir Darna (comptoir marrakech.com) which serves traditional dishes such as *pastilla*.

Shopping for spices in the souks of Marrakech

Day 2

Morning

Start today with a 20-minute walk from Jemaa el-Fna to the Bahia Palace (p32), a 19th-century wonder renowned for its extravagant exterior, intricate mosaics and marble courtyard – leave two hours to explore the palace. When you're finished, walk through the surrounding Mellah district; the name derives from the Arabic word for salt, which Jewish traders dealt in the city. This formerly Jewish quarter now offers a tantalizing mix of spice souks, cobbled alleys, grand synagogues and a large Jewish cemetery. In the neighbouring district, Kasbah (p68), you can explore the Saadian Tombs necropolis (p70), a garden cemetery built in the 16th century. Pause to take in the Chamber of 12 Pillars where a number of the city's Sultans are buried. Near the necropolis, enjoy a simple Moroccan lunch at Café Clock (p73).

SHOP
Just across from the Jardin Majorelle on rue Majorelle, you'll find a host of stylish concept stores selling quality Moroccan products created by independent artisans.

Afternoon

In the afternoon, take a taxi to Guéliz in the New City, where you can stroll past the Jardin Majorelle (see next itinerary) on your way to the nearby Pierre Bergé Museum of Berber Arts (p39). Here you'll find exquisite displays of traditional dress and Amazigh jewellery. Spend a couple of hours exploring the museum, then hop back in a cab to Kabana bar (1 rue Fatima Zahra) in time for sunset cocktails on its leafy roof terrace. From here it's a short stroll to Jemaa el-Fna, where you can sample an array of food options at the night market stalls (p24); we suggest a delightful, slow-cooked tangia.

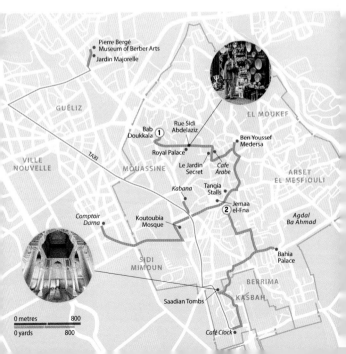

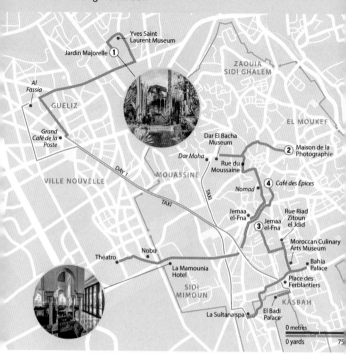

4 DAYS

Day 1

Beat the crowds (and the midday heat) with an early start at the Jardin Majorelle (p38), reserving a good few hours to explore this vast green oasis, which was lovingly landscaped over 40 years. The intense Majorelle blue was patented by the creator of the gardens, Jacques Majorelle, and is now a much-loved colour throughout the world. When you've explored the gardens, pop next door to visit the Yves Saint

> ### 🍵 DRINK
> Enjoy a fresh Moroccan mint tea at Café des Épices, overlooking the Jemaa El-Fna. Traditional tea is made with gunpowder tea and fresh mint, served with extra-large sugar cubes.

Musée Yves Saint Laurent (p39), with fine exhibitions dedicated to the life and work of the French-Algerian fashion designer (buy a combined ticket for the gardens and the museum in advance). Stop for lunch at the iconic Grand Café de la Poste (p85), a great French bistro; the fresh oysters are a popular choice. Come afternoon, take a petit taxi to the El Badi Palace (p36) in the Kasbah; though it's now in ruins, with some imagination you can picture its former extravagance. As evening closes in, recount your day over a candlelit dinner by the pool in Dar Moha's quaint courtyard (darmoha.ma), a former palace.

Day 2

Start your day with a visit to the Maison de la Photographie (p46), which houses

VIEW
The Rooftop Garden at Nobu hotel offers panoramic 360-degree views over the city and Atlas mountains. Enjoy the sunset from one of their poolside tables.

photographs of Morocco over the centuries; it's one of the best ways to get to grips with the country's history. Leave the museum and wander along rue du Moussaine with its chaotic mix of artisan souk stalls and chic boutiques. When you've had your fill of the souks, stop for lunch at Nomad (p79), which offers exquisite views of the Medina. Continue your Medina explorations, skirting back through the souk alleys to Dar el Bacha Museum (p45). This 18th-century palace now displays a varied selection of cultural objects. Meander to Jemaa el-Fna and delight as the square comes to life with performers at sunset.

Day 3

From Jemaa el-Fna, walk 15 minutes south down rue Riad Zitoun el Kdin, one of the main thoroughfares between the Medina and the Kasbah district. This morning, you can hone your cookery skills with a class at the Moroccan Culinary Arts Museum (moroccancam.com). Its three floors

are dedicated to Moroccan cuisine, with daily classes covering the tasty secrets of spice blending and slow cooking. It's been a busy few days, so this afternoon indulge yourself with a luxury *hammam* ritual at nearby La Sultana spa (p49) with its restorative steam rooms and massage options. In the evening, head for a healthy dinner at Al Fassia in Guéliz (p85); this charming Moroccan restaurant is run entirely by women.

Day 4

On your last morning, head to the Medina and grab brunch at Café des Épices (p79). Enjoy the ambience from its terrace with tables overlooking Jemaa el-Fna, the definitive city view. Suitably energized, take a slow stroll along citrus-lined streets to La Mamounia Hotel (p40; you'll pass the souks again for some last-minute souvenir shopping). La Mamounia Hotel opened as a luxury address in the 1920s – you can enjoy a drink by the hotel's pool. Afterwards, walk it off with a brisk stroll around the expansive gardens. This evening, toast your trip with late afternoon cocktails and a sushi dinner on the roof terrace at Nobu (p116), followed by dancing at Théatro in the Hivernage.

Looking out over Jemaa el-Fna at sunset

TOP 10 HIGHLIGHTS

Archway in the Medina

EXPLORE THE
HIGHLIGHTS

There are some sights in Marrakech you simply shouldn't miss, and it's these attractions that make the Top 10. Discover what makes each one a must-see on the following pages.

MUSÉE
PIERRE BERGÉ
DES ARTS BERBÈRES

❶ Jemaa el-Fna

❷ The Night Market

❸ The Souks

❹ Koutoubia Mosque

❺ City Walls and Gates

❻ Bahia Palace

❼ Ben Youssef Medersa

❽ El Badi Palace

❾ Jardin Majorelle

❿ La Mamounia Hotel

ZAOUIA
SIDI GHALEM

ROUTE DES REMPARTS

ASSOUEL

RUE ASSOUEL

RIAD
EL AROUS

7

PLACE
DU MOUKEF

ESSEBTIYNE

MEDINA

PLACE
BEN SALAH

3

ARSET
EL BARAKA

2
1

DOUAR
GRAOUA

ARSET
EL MESFIOULI

Place
Foucault

RUE RIAD ZITOUN EL KEDIM

JNANE
BEN CHAGRA

6

ARSET
MOULAY
MOUSSA

SIDI MIMOUN

PL DES
FERBLANTIERS

8

BERRIMA

0 metres   500
0 yards   500

JEMAA EL-FNA

📍 J3 🏠 Medina

The Medina's central square means "Assembly of the Dead", a reference to a time when the heads of rebels and criminals would be displayed here on spikes. Although nothing so gruesome is on view today, the square is still the nerve centre of Marrakech, populated with some extraordinary sights, including acrobats, storytellers and colourfully costumed water sellers.

1 Orange Juice Stalls
Sellers of freshly squeezed orange juice, with brightly painted barrows, are the first to appear on the square every morning.

2 Porters
With cars banned from crossing Jemaa el-Fna, access to many of the hotels in the surrounding alleys is provided by the ubiquitous *carroser* (porter), who carries travellers' luggage on a wheelbarrow to their riad, guesthouse or hotel in return for a small tip.

TOP TIP

Snake charmers will often try to charge you for holding reptiles.

3 Plants and Herb Stalls
Towards the back of the square, closest to the souks, are a number of small stalls selling a variety of plants and towering piles of herbs. Often overlooked, these stalls add a pop of greenery to Jemaa el-Fna.

4 Acrobats
Acrobats and athletic young people perform spectacular feats to entertain audiences and earn a few coins. Their repertoire usually includes cartwheels, somersaults and tottering pyramids.

5 Herbalists
The herbalists stand as testimony to the Moroccan belief in natural remedies. Compounds of ground roots, dried herbs and various natural products are used for everything from curing colds to warding off the evil eye.

Jemaa el-Fna, Marrakech's main square

6 Fortune-Tellers

Through the day, and especially in the evenings, soothsayers squat beneath umbrellas with packs of tarot cards to read the fortunes of passersby.

7 Café de France

K3 **0524 44 23 19** **7am–11pm daily**

There are several good places to sit and watch the square's hustle and bustle over a cup of coffee, but the raffish air of the Café de France lends it an added appeal, making it a favourite with tourists and locals alike.

8 Music

No matter the time of day or night, music is likely to be heard in the square. The most popular are the Gnawa musicians *(p25)*.

9 Fruit and Nut Stalls

Near the orange juice stalls are vendors selling nuts and dried fruit by weight. Dates, figs and walnuts are a few Moroccan-grown products on offer here.

10 Water Sellers

Known to the locals as *gerrab*, these traditional water sellers roam the square in colourful costumes and tassel-fringed hats, ringing copper bells to announce their arrival. The brass cups are exclusively for Muslims, while the white-metal cups are for everyone else. The water may upset visitors' stomachs.

VIEW

Many cafés set around the Jemaa el-Fna have rooftop terraces, which offer fabulous views of the square and are great people-watching spots.

AN UNPLANNED MASTERPIECE

Jemaa el-Fna square is considered to be a "Masterpiece of the Oral and Intangible Heritage of Humanity" by UNESCO. This is an international list that includes pieces of culture such as song cycles, theatrical traditions and sacred spaces. Inclusion in the list is intended to preserve something unique and irreplaceable.

Clockwise from right **Dried fruit stall on the square; a water seller dressed; enjoying the view from a rooftop terrace overlooking the square**

THE NIGHT MARKET

📍 J3

Every evening as the sun goes down, everyone heads to the aromatic charcoal grills and open-air kitchens of the Night Market, to the east of Jemaa el-Fna, famous for their vast array of Moroccan cuisine. As the air fills with the aroma of flavourful spices, the square throngs with musicians, dancers and storytellers who draw in enthusiastic crowds with their performances late into the night.

1 Khunjul Carts
In the evening, carts are set up in the front of the square with large brass kettles topped up with spicy hot tea. It is said to be a cure-all for any ailment – try a cup.

2 Musicians
A smattering of musicians and groups of Gnawa specialize in hypnotic rhythms and enchanting melodies which set the crowds swaying. Entranced listeners can linger in the square long after everyone else has gone home.

3 Promenade
Once dusk begins to fall, many visitors take a leisurely stroll through the square and along Rue Bab Agnaou. It's an ideal way to unwind and soak in the ambience.

4 Street Food
The ingredients arrive fresh at the market each evening and a wide range of traditional dishes are cooked from scratch in front of you.

EAT
If you find the food stalls to be overwhelming, you can instead head to Argana, on the north side of the square, for pizzas, pastas or salads.

5 Local Flavours
Some of the most popular food offerings here are the varieties of *brochette* – grilled lamb

and chicken – served along with bowls of soup, spicy merguez sausages, grilled fish and bowls of boiled chickpeas. Those feeling adventurous can try the stewed snails.

Local food stall at the market

6 Le Grand Balcon du Café Glacier
☏ 0524 44 21 93
🕓 6am–10:30pm daily

One of the best places to observe the spectacle of the Night Market is the atmospheric rooftop terrace of Le Grand Balcon du Café Glacier. Visit at sunset for superb views.

7 Storytellers
Gifted orators entertain with tales of Islamic heroes. Sessions are in Arabic and often

The many stalls of the Night Market

end on a cliffhanger – the outcome is revealed the following night.

8 Entertainers
Wide-eyed onlookers surround a menagerie of illusionists, performers and fortune-tellers. This is where the Moroccan belief in everyday magic is on full display.

9 Shopping
Walk around to view what's on offer and when you see something you like, just point to what

you want. Prices are usually displayed and everything is fairly inexpensive.

10 Henna Painting
Ladies with piping bags full of henna paste paint hands and feet with intricate designs. Be aware, however, that the paste is often poor quality and can contain ingredients that may cause skin problems. The nearby Marrakech Henna Art Café (p73) offers reputable products.

THE GNAWA
The Gnawa came to Morocco from sub-Saharan Africa. Over the centuries they have kept their culture alive through oral traditions, particularly music. Played on string instruments known as *gimbri*, their music is looping and repetitive, intended to induce an almost trance-like state in the dancers and vocalists. Gnawa music has made a great impact on the global music scene.

THE SOUKS

K2

Marrakech's earliest inhabitants made their living from trade: luxuries like gold and ivory came from the south, while leather, metalwork and ceramics were sent north. Even today, trade continues to be the city's mainstay, with thousands of crafters making a living among the maze of souks that fill much of the northern half of the Medina. Here you will find the most appealing mix of trinkets and treasures.

Spices for sale in Rahba Kedima

1 Rahba Kedima
This open square is home to sellers of traditional herbs and remedies. You may see other objects on display, but these are often just for show.

2 Souk Cherifia
A three-storey mini-market (p78) within the souks, this is the place for edgier finds among a plethora of quirky, designer-owned boutiques. Find designer clothes, bags, jewellery and other handmade accessories here.

3 Souk El Kebir
Found straight on from rue Semmarine, this is the heart of the souks – a narrow alley that lurches from side to side and up and down. It is lined by tiny shops each overflowing with goods, especially leather.

DRINK
Café Arabe (p79), near Souk des Teinturiers, and Café des Epices (p79) in the Rahba Kedima are both great places for some respite.

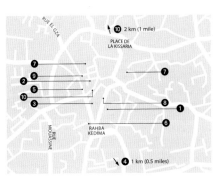

Exploring one of the many souks

sun-dappled alley. Shop owners along Semmarine attempt to entice visitors with a miscellany of robes, kaftans, carpets and unique antiques.

7 Fondouks
The *fondouk* is an ancient hostelry for travelling merchants, built around a courtyard. These days, *fondouks* are workshops or shops.

8 Souk des Tapis
This is the centre of the carpet trade in the city, with a variety of carpets on sale here.

9 Souk des Ferronniers
The sound of clanging and hammering fills the air in this medieval part of the Medina where iron-workers create furniture, lanterns and other home decor items.

10 Souk des Babouches
Every shop and stall here sells nothing but brightly coloured, soft-leather, pointy-toed slippers known as *babouches*. Prices can vary widely between around 60 Dh and 400 Dh, depending on the thickness of the sole, number of layers, presence of a heel and the decoration.

TOP TIP

A tour guide to the souks can be really helpful if you're short of time.

4 Souk El Bab Salaam
This covered market serves the nearby Mellah quarter with everything from food to caged birds.

5 Souk des Teinturiers
Sheaves of freshly dyed wool are hung from ropes strung across one particular alleyway of the dyers' souk (*p75*) for a vibrant, colourful scene.

6 Rue Semmarine
The main route into the souks is via an arch just north of Jemaa el-Fna and along this perpetually busy

Handmade carpets and rugs at a souk

KOUTOUBIA MOSQUE

📍 H4 🏠 Ave Bab Jedid, Medina

Koutoubia's minaret, decorated with flower motifs, is the city's pre-eminent monument, towering above all else, and has always been the first visible sign of Marrakech for travellers approaching from afar. Its iconic status is fitting as the mosque is not only the city's main place of worship, but also one of its oldest buildings. Although access to the mosque is denied to non-Muslims, the nearby gardens are open to all.

1 Koubba Lalla Zohra
This white tomb houses the body of Lalla Zohra, who spent her life in worship and is seen as a saint for her devotion.

2 Mosque of the Booksellers
The Koutoubia was built in 1158. Its name means the Mosque of the Booksellers, a reference to a market that once existed in the neighbourhood.

The minaret of Koutoubia Mosque

TOP TIP
For a look at the prayer hall, peer through an open door on the east wall.

3 Minaret
The minaret is meant to provide a platform from which the muezzin makes the call to prayer. Rather than a simple staircase, the Koutoubia's towering minaret has a spiralling ramp wide enough for a horse to be ridden to the top.

4 The Minaret Decoration
Originally the whole minaret was encased in tiles and stucco, but now only two bands of blue ceramic remain.

5 Koutoubia Gardens
South of the mosque is a garden with a mix of palms and deciduous trees, topiary hedges and colourful roses.

Clockwise from right **Intricate motifs on the minaret's exterior; ruins of the Almohad Mosque; white tomb of Lalla Zohra; attractive Koutoubia gardens**

6 The Mosque Plan

The mosque's plan is rectangular in shape. The main entrance to the east leads to a prayer hall with eight bays and horseshoe arches. North of the prayer hall is a 45-m-(148-ft-) wide courtyard with an ablution fountain and trees.

7 Dar El Hajar

Two wells on the piazza offer a glimpse of the buried remains of the Dar El Hajar (House of Stone), a fortress built by the Almoravids.

VIEW From the Kabana restaurant (*1 rue Fatima Zahra*), you can soak up views of the minaret while enjoying local food.

8 Prayer Times

Exact times of daily prayer change with the seasons, but they are observed five times a day, with sessions held pre-dawn, at noon, late afternoon, at sunset and late evening. The most important prayers of the week are those on Friday at noon.

9 Tomb of Youssef Ben Tachfine

Just north of the mosque, glimpsed through a locked gate, is a walled area with the mausoleum of Youssef Ben Tachfine (1009–1106), tribal leader of the Almoravids and the man credited with the founding of Marrakech.

10 Ruins of the Almohad Mosque

Next to the Koutoubia are the remains of an earlier mosque, built c 1147. The bases of the prayer hall's columns, which are secured behind railings, are clearly visible. They were revealed during excavations by Moroccan archaeologists.

HEIGHTS OF GOOD TASTE

The Koutoubia minaret's continued dominion over the skyline is owed to a piece of legislation imposed by the city's former French colonial rulers. The ruling still holds today; the tower stands 70 m (230 ft) high, in proportions that obey the cannons of Almohad architecture (its height is five times its width).

5

CITY WALLS AND GATES

The city walls date from the 1120s when, under threat of attack from the Almohads of the south, the ruling Almoravid sultan, Ali Ben Youssef, encircled his garrison town with fortifications. Built of pisé, the rose-hued walls get their colour from the earth bricks used to build them. Today, the walls remain largely unchanged, with some 200 look-out towers and a series of 20 gates rising almost 9 m (30 ft) high.

1 Bab Berrima

Apart from serving as perimeter defences, walls and gates were also used to divide up the interior of the Medina. For instance, a wall separated the royal kasbah quarter from the city – Bab Berrima was one of the gates between these two distinct zones. This gate leads to the Medina's main souks.

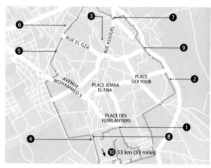

2 Pisé

The walls are built from a mixture of mud, straw and lime (known as pisé), which becomes as hard as brick on drying. The distinctive pinkish-red hue is a result of pigments in the earth.

3 Bab Taghazout

Set at the northern edge of the Medina, the bab (gate) is near to Zaouia of Sidi bel Abbès mosque, a complex centred around a shrine to one of the city's patron saints.

4 Bab er Robb

This was the original southern city gate. The gatehouse building is now occupied by a pottery shop and all foot and car traffic passes through a modern breach in the old walls. The name translates as "Lord's Gate".

5 Bab Doukkala

This massive gate, built by the Almoravids in the 12th century, was the northwestern entrance to the city. It now stands isolated from the walls due to 20th-century urban planning. The cavernous interior of the rooms are perfect for use as an event space.

Pink-hued walls of the Medina

The monumental stone-carved Bab Agnaou city gate

6 Place des 7 Saints

Just outside the north side of the walls stand seven stone towers, each topped by a tree. This giant ensemble pays homage to the seven patron saints of Marrakech.

7 Bab El Khemis

The northernmost gate, this is the most decorative, with a semicircle of stalactite mouldings over the entrance. A lively flea market is held here on Thursdays from 8am to midday.

TOP TIP

As you tour the walls, look up to spot the storks at the highest points.

8 Bab Agnaou

The most beautiful of the city's gates, the "Gate of the Gnawa" is the only stone-built one. It was erected during Almohad sultan Yacoub El Mansour's reign in the 12th century. Although the gate no longer has its towers, the neatly sculpted façade still makes for an impressive sight.

9 Bab Debbagh

This gate gives access to the tanneries, and when it is open, visitors can ascend an internal staircase to the gatehouse roof for sweeping city views. Permission is required to access the roof, which is not always open to visitors.

10 Dar El Haoura

West of the Agdal Gardens, this curious free-standing fortress used to be a garrison for cavalry. Its large horse ramp remains intact to this day.

THE RED CITY

Marrakech's distinctive colouring comes from pigments in the local soil mixed to make the *pisé* from which the city's buildings were traditionally constructed. In the last century, this was threatened by new building materials such as concrete. The ruling French decreed that all new buildings be painted pink – a rule that continues to be enforced today with pleasing aesthetic results.

BAHIA PALACE

📍 K5 🏠 5 rue Riad Zitoun El Jedid 🕐 9am–5pm daily 🌐 bahia-palace.com ↗

The 19th-century Bahia Palace, meaning "Palace of the Favourite" or "Palace of the Beautiful", was constructed by Si Moussa, vizier of Sultan Sidi Mohammed ben Abderrahman, and his son Ba Ahmed, vizier of Moulay Abdelaziz. The palace complex consists of two parts – the older part contains apartments and the newer part has luxurious lodgings. Only a small section of the palace is open to the public.

1 Courtyard of Honour

At the heart of the palace is a 1,500-sq-m (1,800-sq-yd) courtyard. Paved with Italian Carrara marble and *zellij* tilework, it has three fountains with bowls in the centre.

2 Andalucían Garden

Designed in Andalucían style, this garden is split into four sections with a divider that breaks up the quadrants. Plants are arranged by size with smaller ones near the walkway and larger ones towards the back. In the middle of the garden is a fountain.

3 Palace Layout

As you wander through the palace, the influence of different architectural styles can be seen, from Andalucían near the entrance to Persian further back. This is because it was built in stages over many years.

4 School and Mosque

Inside the palace is a Qur'anic school, which was also a mosque, where children living in the palace studied.

Lovely Andalucían-style garden

Courtyard paved with *zellij* tilework

DRINK
Exploring this huge palace is thirsty work. Grab a cold drink from one of the stalls on the north-west corner of place des Ferblantiers.

5 Large Riad
At the north end of the Courtyard of Honour is the Large Riad, which was the original palace of Si Moussa. It has a sleeping area and a private dining area. It is believed the Bahia Palace was the first building in North Africa to use stained glass for decor.

6 Wives' Bedrooms
According to Islamic law, all wives must be treated equally. This is why the four bedrooms, which were built for the sultan's wives, have the exact same proportions. Each bedroom has carved-cedar ceilings.

7 Petit Riad
This area features the Andalucían Garden and a small building, which resembles a tra-ditional Medina house. Inside is the grand Council Chamber.

8 Doors and Windows
It's worth taking time to admire the doors and windows of the palace. The open-arched doors are either plaster carved or wood carved. The windows are a mix-ture of clear glass and stained glass, much of which was imported from Iraq.

9 Council Chamber
This splendid room, featuring lots of stucco and wood work, was the council chamber for Ba Ahmed. It also has a fireplace inlaid with *zellij* tiles.

10 Painted Wooden Ceilings
Intricately painted ceilings, made of cedar wood, are one of the palace's most unique features. Natural dyes from products such as saffron and henna were used to paint the ceilings in a style resembling that used on carpets.

Superb hand-painted wooden ceilings

BEN YOUSSEF MEDERSA

📍 K2 🏛 Place Ben Youssef, Medina 🕐 9am–6pm daily 🌐 medersa benyoussef.ma 📲

This medersa is one of the city's most impressive buildings, and one of the few religious sites to allow entry to non-Muslims. Founded in the 14th century, it was restored and enlarged by the Saadian sultan Moulay Abdellah in around 1565. All the fine decorative detailing that characterizes the peak of Moroccan architecture is on display here.

1 Ablutions Basin
Enter via a long corridor that leads to a square vestibule. On the left is a marble basin carved with floral motifs in the Andalucían style.

2 Dar Bellarj
To the north of the medersa's entrance, Dar Bellarj is a former stork hospital (the name means "House of the Storks"). The building now houses a beautiful cultural centre with a programme of regularly changing exhibitions.

3 Student Cells
Arranged on two levels around the central courtyard are 130 tiny rooms, much like monks' cells. Nearly 900 Muslim students studied in these cells every day until the medersa fell out of use in the 1960s.

4 Chrob ou Chouf Fountain
A little north of the medersa, this handsome fountain is worth seeking out. With a big cedar lintel covered in calligraphy, it is from a time when it was a pious act to provide a public source of clean drinking water. Its name means "drink and look", which implies one should admire its beauty while drinking from it.

Clockwise from below
A student cell; marble columns in the prayer hall; *zellij* tilework in the courtyard; intricately carved plasterwork on the ceiling

Stunning tilework in
the main courtyard

10 Main Courtyard

At the heart of the
medersa is a light-filled
courtyard with arcades
down two sides, a rect-
angular pool in the middle
and a prayer hall. Lined
with elegant galleries,
the courtyard is deco-
rated with traditional
geometric patterns and
Arabic inscriptions carved
in wood and marble.

7 The Role of the Medersa

A medersa was once
a place for religious
instruction, essentially a
theological college. The
students who boarded
here studied the Qur'an
and discussed it with the
institute's *fqih* or imam
(learned religious figures).

5 Carved Stucco

The panels of
intricately carved plaster
that stretch above the
tiling are decorated with
inscriptions or geometric
patterns – depiction of
humans or animals is
prohibited by Islam.

6 Prayer Hall

The elaborate prayer
hall has an octagonal
wooden-domed roof
supported by three
marble columns. The
walls are adorned with
carved stucco deco-
ration and the stucco
features rare palm
motifs and some calligra-
phy of Qur'anic texts.
The room is well lit by
gypsum windows.

8 Tiling

The lowest part
of the courtyard wall
is covered with *zellij*
(glazed tiles) in an eight-
pointed star motif.
Above this is a band
of stylized Qur'anic
text, interwoven with
floral designs.

9 Rue du Souk des Fassis

This winding alley to
the medersa's east is
lined by beautifully
restored fondouks
and old hostels. One
is now a restaurant,
Le Foundouk.

BEN YOUSSEF MOSQUE

The medersa, in its
earlier days, was part
of the complex of the
nearby Almoravid
mosque, which was
founded by Ali Ben
Youssef during his
reign (1106–42).
For several centuries,
this was the focal
point of worship
in the Medina, and,
together with
the medersa, it was
considered a
significant centre
of the Islamic religion
in Morocco.

EL BADI PALACE

⬛ K5 ⬛ Place des Ferblantiers, Medina ⬛ 9am–5pm daily ⬛

Completed in 1603, El Badi Palace was said to be among the most magnificent palaces ever constructed, with walls and ceilings encrusted with gold. The floors are paved with marble and *zellij*, and there is a pool with an island flanked by four sunken gardens. This grand folly survived for all of a century before a conquering sultan stripped the place bare. All that survives now are mudbrick ruins.

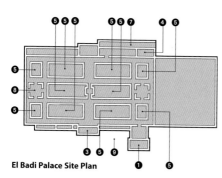

El Badi Palace Site Plan

5 Basins and Gardens

The palace's central courtyard is dominated by five basins and four sunken gardens planted with orange trees. The central basin has an island that comes alive every July for the Festival of Popular Arts. It is also used as a venue during the International Film Festival (*p46*).

1 Mosque Minbar

An "annexe du palais" in the southeast corner displays the 12th-century *minbar* (pulpit) from Koutoubia Mosque. Intricately carved, this is a celebrated artwork of Moorish Spain.

2 Storks

The protrusions in the crumbling walls are well loved by the city storks that have made their nests here. An old Amazigh belief has it that storks are actually transformed humans.

3 Khaysuran Pavilion

A pavilion on the north of the great court and once the palace harem, this space now serves as an exhibition hall, showing work by local and locally based foreign artists.

4 Rooftop Terrace

At the northeastern corner is the only intact tower with a staircase to the roof. At the top, sweeping views make clear the immense size of the complex.

Stork nest on the palace wall

6 Sultan Ahmed El Mansour

The palace was built by El Mansour who became sultan after the Battle of Three Kings (1578), when the Moroccans defeated the Portuguese. Great wealth was accrued from the ransom of Portuguese captives and these riches were poured into the construction of the palace.

TOP TIP

In summer, the palace is a venue for the Marrakech du Rire comedy festival.

Mosaic-tiled floor of the gatehouse

7 The Gatehouse

The original entrance to the palace is found between twin high walls. On its completion, the gatehouse was carved with an inscription glorifying the palace. Now it is a ruin and the complex is entered through a breach in the crumbling walls.

8 Pavilion of 50 Columns

The ruins around the courtyard were probably summer houses. The Koubba El Khamsiniya on the west side is named after the 50 pillars used to build it.

9 Underground Passages

Beside the annexe, there is a path that leads down into the former stables and dungeon, which has four cells where prisoners were kept. These tunnels were also used by the palace staff to conduct their duties without being seen. Though you can still enter, the chambers are only partially lit.

THE BATTLE OF THE THREE KINGS

In an attempt to steal the throne from his uncle, Abdel Malek, the Saadian sultan Abu Abdallah Mohammed II declared war along with King Sebastian of Portugal. All three died in the battle, fought in Ksar El Kebir, between Tangier and Fès. Malek was succeeded by his brother, Ahmed El Mansour, builder of the El Badi Palace.

10 A Sinister Omen

At a banquet to celebrate the palace's completion, a guest declared, "It will make a fine ruin." The omen is now a reality.

Courtyard with sunken gardens and pools

JARDIN MAJORELLE

📍 C4 🏠 Rue Yves Saint Laurent, Guéliz 🕐 9am–6pm daily 🌐 jardinmajorelle.com 🔗

These are the most famous of Marrakech's numerous gardens, and the legacy of an expatriate French painter, Jacques Majorelle. Opened to the public in 1947, the gardens fell into disrepair until 1980, when they were rescued by fashion tycoons and partners Yves Saint-Laurent and Pierre Bergé.

1 The Plants

A beautiful bamboo "forest" and an arid cactus garden with species from around the world share the garden. Most stunning of all are the flowering masses of red and purple bougainvillea.

2 Bassins and Fountains

The garden has a fountain and two large *bassins*, or pools, the smaller of which is fed by a sloping channel. Next to the museum, a third pool is filled with a school of golden carp.

3 Boutique

In the northeast corner, a small boutique sells an interesting selection of quality local handicrafts including clothing, jewellery and miscellaneous leather products such as bags, sandals and beautifully bound notebooks. However, there is a notable paucity of information concerning Majorelle and his garden.

4 Yves Saint Laurent Memorial

The designer, who died in 2008, is remembered by a Roman column, which came from his Tangier home, placed on a red-ochre base. His ashes were scattered around the gardens.

Bamboo groves in the gardens

Majorelle's electric-blue Art Deco villa

7 Majorelle Blue

The name Majorelle lives on in an electrifying shade of cobalt blue – known as "Majorelle blue" – that is widely used in the garden.

8 Galerie Love

The "LOVE" posters Yves Saint Laurent created using collage and sent yearly as New Year's greetings to friends and clients are exhibited here.

9 Musée Yves Saint Laurent

🕙 10am–6pm Thu–Tue
🌐 museeyslmarrakech.com

Situated next door to the Jardin Majorelle, this specially designed modern museum displays some of the legendary French couturier's best-known looks. There is also an arts centre and an auditorium here.

YVES SAINT LAURENT (1936–2008)

French designer Yves Saint Laurent first visited the city in 1962. By the end of the 1960s, he moved into a villa next to the Jardin Majorelle, which he purchased and saved from being turned into an apartment complex. After his death a small memorial column was placed in the gardens. The Musée Yves Saint Laurent opened in late 2017 as a tribute to the designer.

10 Pierre Bergé Museum of Berber Arts

Jacques Majorelle's garden-villa-studio is now a museum dedicated to the Amazigh people. More than 600 items illustrate aspects of their traditional culture.

DRINK
There is a pleasant café on site that has a great menu of breakfast and lunch dishes, as well as various refreshing beverages to choose from.

5 Jacques Majorelle

French artist Jacques Majorelle (1886–1962) came to Morocco in 1917 to recuperate from heart problems. He immediately saw the painterly potential of southern Morocco and fell in love with the place.

6 Majorelle's Paintings

The museum's first room has a series of lithographs depicting various Atlas kasbahs. Some of Majorelle's most acclaimed works are the stunning tourism posters that he created for Morocco.

Visitors at Musée Yves Saint Laurent

LA MAMOUNIA HOTEL

📍 H5   🏠 Ave Bab Jedid, Medina   🌐 mamounia.com

One of the world's great old hotels, La Mamounia has been welcoming the rich and famous since it opened its doors in 1923. Originally built as a palace in the 19th century for the crown prince of Morocco, it was turned into a hotel for the Moroccan railways by the French. Set within 7 ha (17 acres) of delightful gardens, it is surrounded by the city's 12th-century red-ochre ramparts.

European-style gardens at the hotel

1 The Gardens
The hotel's acres of formal European-style gardens were laid out for Prince Al-Mamoun and predate the construction of the hotel. Well-manicured paths, lined with citrus trees, fragrant rose blossoms and ancient olive groves, lead between ponds and flowerbeds to a central pavilion. The gardens are also open to non guests.

2 The Architects
The original French architects Henri Prost and Antoine Marchisio of La Mamounia blended Art Deco with traditional Moroccan motifs. In 1986, major renovations were carried out by the designers of Morocco's royal palaces, further changing the character of the building.

3 The Centenary Chandelier
Also known as the Jewel of the Grande Dame, this dazzling chandelier is the centre piece of the hotel's lobby. Commissioned to mark La Mamounia's centenary in 2023, it resembles two traditional Amazigh necklaces.

4 Famous Guests
Since the 1950s, the hotel has welcomed a number of noteworthy people from the political and entertainment worlds. The likes of British Prime Minister Winston Churchill, US Presidents Franklin D Roosevelt, Ronald Reagan and Bill Clinton, and South African President Nelson Mandela have stayed here, as have stars from French cinema and Hollywood, including Charlie Chaplin, Francis Ford Coppola, Nicole Kidman and Kate Winslet.

5 The Rooms
Many of the rooms in this landmark hotel have been luxuriously renovated using wood and leather in warm Moroccan shades.

6 The Suites
The most famous of the hotel's several grand suites is the one named after Winston Churchill. The decoration and furnishings, such as the tartan armchairs, are intended to evoke the politician's era.

La Mamounia's grand courtyard

> 🛍 **SHOP**
> La Boutique Mamounia is a great place to pick up fine jewellery, dresses and fragrances crafted with citrus picked from the hotel gardens.

The suite also contains several artifacts, including Churchill's pipe.

7 Churchill Bar

"This is a wonderful place, and the hotel one of the best I have ever used" were the words Winston Churchill used in a letter to Clementine, his wife, to describe the hotel and the city that he adored. The hotel's bar, housed in a luxurious Pullman carriage in honour of the hotel's famous railway past, is named after him.

> **TOP TIP**
>
> Casually dressed visitors may be denied entry to the hotel.

8 Churchill's Paintings

Winston Churchill was so at home at the hotel that he often painted in the afternoon. A couple of his paintings are still on display in the hotel.

9 Majorelle Ceiling

Winston Churchill met fellow painter Jacques Majorelle in the winter of 1946 during one of his many stays at La Mamounia. The politician persuaded the hotel's management to commission a mural by Majorelle, which you can now see on the ceiling of the extended lobby. Today, the Frenchman is best known in the city for his creative masterpiece, the beautiful Jardin Majorelle *(p38)*.

Drinks served at the Churchill Bar

10 The Man Who Knew Too Much

Several scenes of this 1956 Alfred Hitchcock thriller, featuring James Stewart and Doris Day, were shot in La Mamounia, as well as other locations across the city.

TOP 10 OF EVERYTHING

Jardin Majorelle

MOROCCAN ARCHITECTURE

1 Stucco Plaster
A decorative element of Moroccan architecture, carved plaster can cover entire walls in fantastic design. The work is executed by crafters while the plaster is still damp – the patterns are sketched onto the surface, then gouged out with hammer and chisel.

2 Pigeonholes
The numerous pigeonholes peppering the walls in the city are, in reality, remnants of wooden scaffolding used to erect walls.

3 Tadelakt Plaster
Known for its decorative and water-resistant properties, this traditional technique was initially used in bathhouses to counter the heat and moisture. Walls are treated with a limestone plaster, which, once set, is polished with flat stones, then glazed with egg whites and polished again with local black soap made from olives. The finished surface looks akin to soft leather, with a delightful satin sheen.

4 Carved Woodwork
Although some of the same designs are used to decorate both plaster and wood, the latter often has inscriptions in Arabic, the sacred language in which the Qur'an was revealed to the Prophet Mohammed. The inscriptions are of a religious nature and invariably praise the glory of Allah. They are both decorative and informative.

5 Fountains
Fountains and basins are required for ritual ablutions before prayers. With such an arid climate, the provision of drinking water is also seen as a charitable act.

6 Courtyards
A distinctive feature of Islamic architecture is its focus on the interior rather than the exterior, which is generally windowless. Courtyards serve as air-wells into which the cool night air sinks. They also allow women to enjoy the outdoors without having to cover up.

Courtyard at El Badi Palace

Colourful *zellij* tiles with geometric patterns

7 Zellij Tiling

One of the most striking features of Moroccan architecture is its use of small, multicoloured tiles laid in complex geometric patterns. This is known as the *zellij* technique, where tiles are created as large squares and then hand-cut into smaller shapes. Conventional shapes and sizes are typically used, though there are as many as 360 different types of pieces.

8 Square Minarets

The square design of Moroccan minarets can be traced to the Umayyad rulers of Islamic Spain, who were of Syrian origin. Syrians are almost unique in the Middle East for their square minarets, probably influenced by the church towers built by Syrian Christians.

9 Pisé

The basic building material used in Morocco, *pisé* is wet earth that is mixed with straw and gravel pounded between two parallel boards and strengthened by lime. If it is not made well, the mixture can cause the structure to crumble in the rain – southern Morocco is littered with semi-melted buildings.

10 Horseshoe Arches

Properly known as *outrepassé* arches, these are where the arch curves back inwards after its widest point, to give an effect like a keyhole or horseshoe. This design is most commonly associated with Moorish Spain and North Africa.

TOP 10 HISTORIC BUILDINGS

1. Dar Si Saïd Museum
🅚 K4
The 19th-century Dar Si Saïd serves as a museum of decorative arts. It is temporarily closed for restoration following an earthquake in 2023.

2. Koutoubia Mosque
Marrakech's biggest and tallest minaret *(p28)* can be found here.

3. El Badi Palace
Its *pisé* walls *(p36)* are in an advanced state of dilapidation with "pigeonholes".

4. Bahia Palace
This 19th-century palace *(p32)* features a riot of *zellij* work.

5. Ben Youssef Medersa
This structure *(p34)* displays an array of decorative elements, including fine *zellij* work.

6. La Mamounia Hotel
Built in 1923, La Mamounia Hotel is known for its splendid Art Deco and Moorish architecture.

7. Almoravid Koubba
The earliest example of Islamic architecture *(p77)* in Marrakech with beautifully carved plasterwork.

8. Dar Cherifa
This townhouse *(p47)* has an example of a courtyard with some extraordinary carved woodwork.

9. Dar El Bacha
🅚 J2
Enough dazzling, multicoloured patterned *zellij* tiling to make your head spin.

10. Bab Agnaou
This gate *(p31)* into the kasbah quarter is an impressive keyhole arch.

Dar El Bacha

ARTS AND CULTURE

1 David Bloch Gallery
🅾 B5 🅰 17 rue de Yougoslavie, Guéliz 🕐 By appointment only
🌐 davidblochgallery.com

To see the new face of Marrakech art, visit this stylish gallery specializing in contemporary Moroccan art and graffiti.

2 Maison de la Photographie
🅾 K2 🅰 46 rue Souh Ahal Fassi, Medina 🕐 9:30am–7pm daily
🌐 maisondelaphotographie.ma

This is a small museum dedicated to photographs taken by travellers to Morocco from the late 19th century to the 1960s. It occupies a beautiful old courtyard house which is not far from the Ben Youssef Medersa. The rooftop café is a refreshing place to stop for a glass of mint tea and take in the view.

3 Marrakech International Film Festival
🌐 festivalmarrakech.info

Sponsored by movie fan King Mohammed VI, the festival was launched in 2001 and is held in December. A number of stars have graced the red carpet, including Martin Scorsese and Willem Dafoe.

4 Musée d'Art et de Culture de Marrakech (MACMA)
🅾 C5 🅰 61 rue de Yougoslavie, Guéliz 🕐 10am–7pm Mon–Sat 🌐 musee macma.com

This elegant gallery displays works by artists who fell in love with Marrakech including Jacques Majorelle, Eugène Delacroix and Raoul Dufy. Temporary exhibitions highlight Moroccan artists.

5 Galerie 127
🅾 B5 🅰 127 ave Mohammed V, Guéliz 🕐 3–7pm Thu–Sat 🌐 galerie 127.com

The first gallery in North Africa devoted to contemporary photography, this white-walled space in the district of Guéliz exhibits a range of works by local and international photographers from all over the world.

Harem musicians (c 1930), Maison de la Photographie

losing ceremony at the Marrakech
nternational Film Festival

6 Dar Cherifa

📍 J2 🌐 marrakech-riads.com/
restaurant-dar-cherifa

This 16th-century townhouse is
a cultural centre that hosts regular
exhibitions, with Gnawa musicians
(025) often performing on opening
nights. The small library offers art
and heritage books to browse while
enjoying tea or coffee.

7 Galerie SINIYA28

📍 B5 🏠 28 rue Tarik Ibn Ziad
🕐 10:30am–1pm & 2:30–7pm Mon–
Sat 🌐 galeriesiniya28.com

The exhibits at this modern art gallery
focus on representing both Moroccan
and international up-and-coming artists.

8 Mouassine Museum of Music

📍 J2 🏠 4–5 derb el Hammam,
Mouassine 🕐 10am–6pm daily
🌐 museedelamusique.ma 🔌

A former home of a 16th-century
Saadian noble, this is one of the
city's most delightful museums, with
the family's living quarters carefully
restored. The museum, housed in the
attic, has exhibits on Moroccan music
and hosts regular musical performances.

9 Marrakech Street Art

Throughout Marrakech you will
see graffiti art on the walls. Some are
remnants from the Marrakech Biennale,
a former arts festival, while others
have been commissioned over the
years. Adorning a wall directly across
from the Marrakech train station is a
large image of an older local man by
German artist Hendrik Beikirch.

10 Marrakech National Festival of Popular Arts

🌐 fnap.ma

Troupes from all over Morocco
perform at this celebration of
Amazigh music and dance held
every year in June or July.

TOP 10 MOROCCAN CULTURAL FIGURES

1. Tahar Ben Jelloun
Morocco's best-known French-based
writer won the French Prix Goncourt
in 1987 for his novel *The Sacred Night*.

2. Mahi Binebine
This Marrakech-based artist authored
the excellent *Welcome to Paradise*.

3. Hassan Hajjaj
The graphic artist behind the T-shirts
worn by the staff at London's famous
Moroccan restaurant, Momo.

4. Laïla Marrakchi
This Casablanca-born film-maker's
debut feature, *Marock,* caused a
scandal on its release in 2006.

5. Farid Belkahia
Famous for painting on lamb-skin
canvases, Belkahia, one of Morocco's
most influential artists, died in 2014.

6. Jamel Debbouze
Known for his role in *Amélie*, this
French-Moroccan actor also runs the
Marrakech du Rire comedy festival.

7. Elie Mouyal
This architect is hugely popular among
celebrities looking for a fancy residence.

8. Master Musicians of Jajouka
International fame came upon this
musical ensemble from a north
Moroccan village, courtesy of the
Rolling Stones.

9. Leila Abouzeid
The first female Moroccan author to
have her work translated into English.

10. Hassan Hakmoun
Based in New York, this trance specialist
performed on Jemaa el-Fna as a child.

Hassan
Hakmoun

HAMMAMS AND SPAS

1 Heritage Spa

H2 · 40 Arset Aouzal, Bab Doukkala, Medina · 10am–8pm daily · heritagespamarrakech.com

A modern spa with a wide variety of treatments and packages at reasonable prices, the Heritage is extremely friendly and has English-speaking staff. It is an ideal option if you have never experienced a *hammam* before.

2 Les Bains de Marrakech

J6 · 2 derb Sedra, Mechouar Bab Agnaou, Kasbah · 9am–7pm daily · lesbainsdemarrakech.com

This popular spa provides a dazzling selection of treatments such as water massage, shiatsu massage and the intriguingly named "four-handed massage". The *hammam* treatments typically last 45 minutes. Unusually, the *hammam* offers small, mixed steam-bath cubicles (swimsuits are compulsory).

3 Hammam Ziani

K4 · Rue Riad Zitoun el Jedid, Medina · 9am–10pm daily

Located near the Bahia Palace, this *hammam* offers all the facilities that you would expect (scrub, soak, steam and pummel) in surroundings that are significantly cleaner than those found in other Medina bathhouses.

The Winter Courtyard at Riad Noir d'Ivoire

4 Marajah Spa

H2 · Las Torres de Majorelle Building, Blvd de Safi 69 · 10am–10pm daily · marajahspa.com

Located near the Jardin Majorelle, this spa is a popular mid-range option with a wide range of services. It also has a well-equipped kids spa for 6–12-year-olds, offering an indulgent chocolate scrub massage.

5 La Maison Arabe

The *hammams* housed in larger riads and hotels are often restricted to guests, but not at La Maison Arabe *(p114)*. Book yourself in for a vigorous *gommage* (rubdown) with a *kissa* (loofah mitten) and follow it up with a soothing back, face or foot massage.

6 Hammam El Bacha

H3 · 20 rue Fatima Zohra, Medina · Men: 7am–1pm daily; women: 1–9pm daily

One of the city's most historic *hammams*, this spot is thronged by tourists as well as the locals. The staff of the Dar El Bacha, just across the road, were its first patrons. The highlight is an impressive 6-m (20-ft) cupola in the steam room. It offers a range of facials, manicures, henna treatments and oil massages.

Cosy interior of the Hammam Ziani

7 Riad Noir d'Ivoire

🗺 K3 🏠 31–33 derb Jdid, Bab Doukhala 🌐 noir-d-ivoire.com

This hip riad includes Coco's Spa, which offers a *hammam* and spa treatments such as an hour-long massage in front of a fire.

8 Royal Mansour

As ornate and opulent as the five-star hotel (*p115*) itself, the Royal Mansour is exquisite. The white wrought-iron atrium brings to mind a giant bird enclosure – complete with the sound of birdsong. Sprawling across three floors, the spa also includes a large indoor swimming pool as well as a fitness centre.

9 Farnatchi Spa

🗺 K2 🏠 2 derb Farnatchi, Medina 🌐 farnatchispa.com

The day spa located next to La Farnatchi (*p115*) is exquisitely designed, with private marble *hammams* featuring vaulted ceilings and a courtyard café for lunch. Visitors can even hire the whole spa for the day. Combine a body scrub treatment with an aromatic mask and finish with a *beldi* massage using black soap.

10 La Sultana

A historic five-star hotel (*p114*) next to the Saadian Tombs, La Sultana offers a high-end hammam experience. It has a beautiful basement spa complete with a luxurious star-domed marble Jacuzzi, a *hammam*, balneotherapy baths, open-air massage cabins and a solarium. Packages include traditional Moroccan treatments, massages with locally sourced essential oils, aromatherapy and seaweed treatments. It gets busy so make sure you book well in advance.

Relaxing in the spa at La Sultana hotel

PARKS AND GARDENS

Diverse array of plant life at Jardin Majorelle

1 Jardin Majorelle

Formerly owned by designer Yves Saint Laurent (p39), these world-renowned gardens (p38) were first created by expatriate French artist Jacques Majorelle. Though small, they are quite lovely, with bamboo groves, cacti, palms and pools floating with water lilies. The artist's former studio is now a museum, painted in a searing blue colour that is widely known as "Majorelle blue". The museum has more than 600 items, which illustrate aspects of traditional Amazigh culture.

2 La Mamounia Gardens

Landscaped with beautiful roses, blossoming jacarandas, Madagascar periwinkle and bougainvilleas along with olive and citrus groves, in perfectly organized avenues, the Arset El Mamoun gardens predate La Mamounia Hotel (p40). They were established in the 18th century by Prince Moulay Mamoun, laid out around a central pavilion that served as a royal residence. Hidden in the grounds is also a wonderful garden with a wide range of herbs and vegetables.

3 Le Jardin Secret

📍 J2 🏠 121 rue Mouassine, Medina 🕐 Hours vary, chech website 🌐 lejardin secretmarrakech.com 🔗

Opened to the public in 2016, this large courtyard garden is in the middle of the Medina. Pleasant rather than spectacular, it is a fine place to relax with a mint tea.

4 Musée de la Palmeraie

📍 F4 🏠 Dar Tounsi, route de Fes 🕐 9am–6pm daily 🌐 benchaabane.com/musee_palmeraie

This harmonious blend of nature and culture is set in a vast palm oasis (the Palmeraie) on the edge of town. The museum exhibits contemporary Moroccan art. There are also several fine thematic gardens inhabited by tortoises, turtles and frogs.

5 Menara Gardens

📍 B7 🏠 Ave de la Menara, Hivernage 🕐 9am–5pm daily 🌐 jardin-menara.com

Laid out in the 12th century, the Menara Gardens, with their orchard, pool and pavilion, epitomize a typical Islamic garden. The large pool is overlooked by a green-tile-roofed pavilion.

Menara Gardens, with the High Atlas mountains the background

0 metres 1,000
0 yards 1,000

ROUTE D'EL JADIDA

ROUTE DE SAFI

AVENUE DU 11 JANVIER

3 km
(2 miles) **4**

VILLE NOUVELLE

RUE EL GZA

RUE ASSOUEL

PLACE DU 16 NOVEMBRE

PLACE DE LA LIBERTÉ

AVE DU PRÉSIDENT KENNEDY

AVE MOHAMMED V

3 MEDINA

AVENUE HASSAN II

8

GUÉLIZ

BLVD MOHAMMED VI

7

PLACE JEMAA EL FNA

9

HIVERNAGE

AVENUE DE LA MENARA

EL YARKOUB

PLACE DES FERBLANTIERS

2

Bab Jedid
Olive Grove

ROUTE 501

KASBAH

5

Menara Gardens

200 km
(124 miles) **10**

30 km
(19 miles) **6**

6 Anima Garden

📍 C1 🚪 Douar Sbiti, Route d'Ourika 🕐 9am–6pm daily
🌐 anima-garden.com 💶

Artist André Heller's Anima Garden features local flowers and trees interspersed with funky sculpture elements. The garden is a haven of peace, tranquility and beauty, perfect for escaping the hustle and bustle of the city. There is an on-site café, which is a great place to sit with a drink and soak up the views. Tickets can be purchased online and a shuttle service from the city is available.

7 Cyber Parc Arsat Moulay Abdeslem

📍 G3 🚪 Ave Mohammed V
🕐 7:30am–6:30pm daily

This public garden, between avenue Mohammed V and the walls of the Medina, has been given a makeover. The lawns, divided by palm-shaded pathways, are a favourite lunch spot. The park also has free Wi-Fi hot spots.

8 Jnane El Harti

Pretty and often quiet, this neatly planted green space *(p82)* is beloved by locals, with its proximity to places of work making it a favourite lunchtime hangout.

9 Koutoubia Gardens

On the south side of the landmark mosque *(p28)*, these gardens have pathways lined with flowerbeds and topiary hedges. The roses seem impervious to the heat and bloom throughout the year.

10 Dar al Hossoun

📍 B2 🚪 Taroudant 🌐 alhossoun.com

The desert gardens at Hossoun, a guesthouse in the town of Taroudant in southern Morocco, contain more than 900 different species of plants. The gardens can be booked for private tours.

The beautiful Jardin Majorelle

OFF THE BEATEN TRACK

1 Jarjeer Donkey Sanctuary
🅿 C1 🏠 Rue d'Amizmiz 🌐 jarjeer.org

Jarjeer is a retirement home, care centre and orphanage for mules and donkeys in a beautiful valley in the foothills of the Atlas Mountains. There is a coffee shop here and the purchases help to support the sanctuary. It is 24 km (15 miles) from Marrakech on the Route d'Amizmiz, near Oumnass village.

2 Rock Climbing
Rock climbing is popular with visitors to Marrakech. Whether you're an expert climber or a keen beginner, Climb Morocco (climbmorocco.com) offers rock climbing routes and excursions in the Marrakech area and beyond. This outdoor activity is open to all ages and skill levels, and guides, equipment and training are provided to make sure you have a great and safe experience.

3 Sidi Ghanem
🅿 C1 🏠 219 Quartier Industriel Sidi Ghanem 🌐 sidi-ghanem.com

Anyone serious about shopping for homeware and interior decor items (candles, pottery, linen, furniture) should head to this industrial estate on the northern fringes of town, which has become the city's "design district". It is home to more than a dozen fantastic shops (start with Maison Fenyadi) and has a scattering of cafés and restaurants for between-purchase sustenance.

4 Lalla Takerkoust
Head out of the city to the town of Lalla Takerkoust (p96) to lose the crowds. Here, you can soak up the superb mountain views and enjoy canoeing and dune-gazing. There are also hiking trails leading out to the surrounding countryside.

Tombstones at the Miâara Jewish Cemetery

5 Miâara Jewish Cemetery
🅿 L5 🏠 Ave Taoulat El Miara

In the early 20th century there were around 36,000 Jews living in Marrakech, but now there are only maybe a couple of hundred. Evidence of this lost populace can be seen at this sprawling, 200-year-old walled cemetery in the little-visited southeast corner of the Medina.

6 La Pause
🅿 C1 🏠 Douar Lmih Laroussiene, Agafay 🌐 lapause-marrakech.com

Another option for getting out of the city, this lodge is set in the arid Agafay valley about 40 minutes southwest of Marrakech. It is a chic eco-resort offering a choice of accommodation – nomad tents strewn with Amazigh rugs and cushions, or partially open huts made of pisé. There are plenty of fun activities on offer, including swimming, horse trekking, pétanque and golf.

7 Marché Central

Set away from the Medina, just east of place du 16 Novembre and behind the modern shopping centre, this market (p84) is where locals and the city's expats do their shopping. Mixed in with the food stalls are a handful of craft shops where both quality and price tend to be better than the souks.

8 Souk El Khemis

D4 **Bab el Khemis**

Entrepreneurs renovating riads scout this flea market just north of the Medina walls for unusual finds, including carved doors and other bits of recycled handiwork.

9 Palmeraie Palace

F4 **Circuit de la Palmeraie**
rotana.com

This palm grove north of the city is the favoured retreat of the rich. Among the secluded villas are also several upmarket hotels, including the Palmeraie – one of North Africa's leading golf resorts. There are also several restaurants and bars as well as a free kids' club.

10 Beldi Country Club

C1 **Route de Barrage**
beldicountryclub.com

Escape the dust and chaos of the Medina to this chic rural retreat just beyond the city centre. Among shaded olive groves and rose gardens are restaurants, pools, a tennis court and a spa. Visitors can book cooking and pottery lessons, and the site also includes a luxurious hotel for overnight stays.

Outdoor pool at the charming Palmeraie Palace

FAMILY ATTRACTIONS

1 Jemaa el-Fna
Come sunset, the Medina's main square (p22) turns into a full-scale circus replete with acrobats, musicians, magicians and other entertainers lighting up the streets. You can grab front row seats for this open-air theatre at one of the square's café terraces.

2 Parks and Gardens
The cities' tropical walled gardens are perfect for running off excess energy. Quirky Anima Garden (p51) is an interactive park with abstract sculptures and installations (the giant heads spraying water are particular favourites). Children go free at Jardin Majorelle (p38), and they'll love exploring the unusual cacti and fountains.

3 Motorcycle Tours
Hop on board a sidecar motorbike and allow a Marrakech Insiders (marrakechinsiders.com) guide to take you on a tailor-made tour of the city. Vehicles are furnished with a chic vintage look, and each bike accommodates a driver guide plus two passengers. For those who like unusual modes of transport, as well as seeing different sides of the city, these tours are a win.

4 Waterparks
Keep the kids cool at one of the cities' excellent waterparks. Oasiria, south of Marrakech, is home to the largest wave pool in Africa, as well as a lazy river, a kid's club and chill-out cabanas (oasiria.com); a free shuttles run from Jemaa el-Fna and Guéliz. Alternatively, pool day passes are available for most of the cities' pools.

5 Water Museum
◘ C1 ◘ Circuit de la Palmeraie – Route de Casablanca ◘ 9am–7pm daily ◘ watermuseums.net
Morocco might be largely arid, but water has played a huge and complex role in the country's history. This unique museum explores Morocco's relationship with water over the centuries, with interactive maps and videos educating kids on sustainable futures. Educational, impactful and (dare we say) fun.

Street performers dressed
in costumes at Jemaa el-Fna

6 Arts and Crafts
At the Lamsaty Handmade
workshop (*lamsatyhandmade.com*),
children can hone their pottery,
painting and embroidery skills, taking
their cue from Morocco's rich artisanal
traditions. Pre-booking is required.

7 Indoor Play Areas
When the heat becomes too
oppressive, it's customary for Marrakchi
families to make the most of the city's
wide range of air-conditioned play
centres, which are found in most malls
and service stations. Kawkab Jeux (*rue el
Imam Chafii*) in Guéliz has indoor and
outdoor play areas with bouncy castles,
soft play and trampolines, plus a café.

8 Henna
Get hands on with one of
Morocco's most beautiful cultural
traditions through the art of henna.
The Marrakech Henna Art Café (*p73*)
offers 100 per cent natural henna
tattoos; their catalogue includes both
traditional and animal designs which
are sure to win over younger travellers.

9 Agafay Desert
Head 30 km (18 miles) south of the
city and you'll find yourself in the desert
wonderland of the Agafay (*p65*). This
wide expanse of scorched sand offers a
fascinating insight into Morocco's desert
culture, which is best discovered during
an overnight stay with Caravan Agafay
(*ourhabitas.com*) or an e-bike tour.

10 Ourika Valley
C2
Nestled in the heart of the Atlas
Mountains, the Ourika Valley offers
hiking trails to suit the whole family.
Combine a short trail from either Khemis
or Asguine with a river swim and picnic
lunch near the region's waterfalls.

**Enjoying the wave pool
at Oasiria waterpark**

TOP 10 ACTIVITIES

1. Cooking
Souk Cuisine (*soukcuisine.com*)
organizes culinary weeks or tailor-
made programmes.

2. Cycling
Bicycles can be hired across the city.
Pikala Bikes (*pikalabikes.com*) offers
both rentals and bike tours.

3. Golf
Play at the Palmeraie Palace (*p55*) or
the Golf d'Amelkis (*golfamelkis.com*).

4. Hot-Air Ballooning
Marrakech By Air (*marrakechbyair.com*)
offers early morning balloon rides over
the desert.

5. Tennis
The Royal Tennis Club (*0524 43 19 02*)
welcomes non-members.

6. Karting
Atlas Karting (*0661 23 76 87*) on
the Route de Safi also offers quad
bike rides.

7. Mountain Biking
In addition to full-on rough-terrain
biking, MBA (*marrakechbikeaction.com*)
offers city rides.

8. Marathons
A marathon and a half marathon
(*marathon-marrakech.com*) take place
in January.

9. Indoor Rock Climbing
Atlas Elevation (*atlaselevation.com*)
offers wall climbing and bouldering
for all ages.

10. Quad Biking
A thrilling experience for all – Dunes
and Desert (*dunesdesert.com*) is one
of many offering quad bike adventures.

Quad biking in the desert

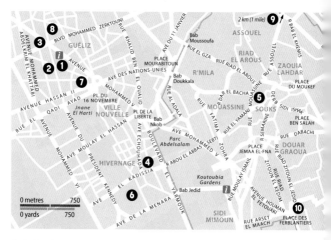

NIGHTS OUT

1 MY Kechmara

This hip café-bar (p85) has a friendly, relaxed vibe. In addition to live music and art installations, there is beer on tap and a large food menu.

2 Sky Bab

B5 ⌂ Cnr blvd Mansour Eddahbi and rue Mohammed El Beqqal, Guéliz ⓦ babhotel marrakech.ma

This rooftop bar, found at the stylish Bab Hotel in central Guéliz, is spacious and cool in every sense of the word. There are DJs at the weekend and, on occasion, live music.

3 Sky Bar

B5 ⌂ 89 Angle bld Zerhtouni and Mohammed V, Guéliz
Situated on the roof of La Renaissance Hotel, this is one of the most buzzing bars in town. Seven storeys above Place Abdel Moumen Ben Ali, it offers terrific views down Mohammed V back to the Medina. On a clear day, you can see the Atlas mountains.

4 Comptoir Darna

A spacious lounge located above the ground-floor restaurant (p85), with a long cocktail bar, this is the place where everyone dresses up for the evening. The atmosphere is sophisticated and elegant. There are also exciting nightly shows featuring dance troupes, Gnawa singers (p25) or orchestras performing traditional Arab music.

Casual lounge area at Comptoir Darna

5 Café Arabe
Due to the presence of several saints' shrines, the serving of alcohol in the Medina is severely restricted, limited to just a handful of venues that predominantly cater to foreign travellers. The casual Café Arabe (p79) serves Moroccan and Italian food but you can drink without eating on one of its terraces or in the courtyard.

6 Théatro
⊡ C6 **⌂** Hotel Es Saadi, ave El Kadissia, Hivernage **⊙** 11pm–5am daily **▥** theatromarrakech.com
Set in a converted music hall, this chic, popular nightclub is known for its uproarious hedonism. The former stage is now a busy dance floor, with a full schedule of resident and international DJs, and hip-hop acts. Advance booking is recommended.

7 Baromètre
⊡ B4 **⌂** Rue Moulay Ali, Guéliz **⊙** 6:30pm–1am Mon–Sat **▥** lebaro metre.net
Cocktail lovers won't be disappointed with a visit to this basement bar where mixologists create innovative drinks. Ask for a custom cocktail to be made for you or choose from the selection of classic ones on offer. Baromètre also has a restaurant that serves great food.

Diners at the elegant Grand Café de la Poste

8 Grand Café de la Poste
This beautifully converted villa was originally a French-colonial-era post office, which was built in 1925. Often compared to Rick's Café in Casablanca, it has a brasserie-like feel and does a busy lunch and dinner trade. The menu features French classics and the wine list is excellent. In the early evening, the terrace out front is the ideal place for a sundowner by the place du 16 Novembre.

9 Nikki Beach
⌂ Circuit de la Palmeraie **⊙** Mar–Jan: 11:30am–8pm daily **▥** palmeraieresorts.com
Lounge by the pool and swim out to the "floating bars" at this glitzy club just 15 minutes from the Medina. Although it closes at 8pm, this is a popular spot for an early-evening drink.

10 Kosybar
Located in the heart of the Medina, this establishment (p73) features a ground floor with a piano and an elegant bar, plus a first floor with cosy nooks. Head to the roof terrace for picturesque views of the stork nests around the wall of the El Badi Palace and Koutoubia Mosque.

LOCAL DISHES

1 Tajines
Cooked slowly at a low temperature in a clay pot with a cone-shaped lid that gives the dish its name, a tajine typically combines meat with fruits. Ingredients for these stewed dishes include any foodstuff that braises well, such as fish, beef, dried fruits, olives and vegetables.

2 Moroccan Salads
Moroccan salads are traditionally part of a meal. Usually, one to three different small salads are served. These are made up of fresh vegetables, such as carrots, bell peppers, courgette and tomatoes.

3 Mint Tea
The ubiquitous green tea made with fresh mint leaves is invariably served with vast quantities of sugar.

Moroccan sweet mint tea

The technique of pouring is almost as crucial as the drink itself; the long, curved teapot spout allows the tea to be poured theatrically, and the tradition is to have three glasses each.

4 Breads
There are various types of breads available that are traditionally served with every meal. *Khobz* (a small round loaf) generally accompanies a main dish, while *msemmen* (flatbread) is served for breakfast. The *rghaif* (bread stuffed with beef and spices) is also a popular afternoon snack.

5 Briouats
Briouats are small triangles of delicious filo pastry filled with a variety of flavours, the most common being spiced minced lamb with pine nuts and feta cheese with spinach. Some kitchens in Marrakech also prepare them with shrimp, chicken and lemon. A sweet version of the dish, filled with groundnuts and soaked in honey, is also widely available.

6 Couscous
A staple cuisine across North Africa, couscous comprises tiny grains of semolina that are steamed, causing them to swell and turn light and fluffy. Couscous is usually eaten with a spicy, harissa-flavoured broth and served with a variety of steamed vegetables and meat.

elicious tajine in local
ood stalls

7 Tangia

This meat-heavy dish was born in the souks of Marrakech by workmen. It is an iconic dish of slow-cooked lamb or beef with preserved lemons, garlic and saffron.

8 Harira

A traditional Moroccan soup made with tomatoes, lentils, chickpeas, spices and lamb, this is a substantial meal by itself. Associated with special occasions, it is also served during Ramadan.

9 Moroccan Pastries

The popular honey cakes or *chabakia*, deep-fried and dipped in honey, are served during Ramadan. Another treat is sweet *pastilla* – a filo pastry covered in nuts and *crème anglaise* (custard).

10 Pastilla

Eaten both as a starter as well as a main dish, *pastilla* is a pillow of filo pastry filled with a sweet and savoury stuffing, generally shredded chicken or pigeon. The dish is dusted all over with cinnamon and sugar for a distinctive Moroccan flavour.

Pastilla, a traditional sweet Moroccan pastry

TOP 10 **VARIATIONS ON A TAJINE**

Beef tajine

1. Beef with fennel and peas
The chefs at La Maison Arabe's restaurant (p79) make good use of beef in this extremely tasty tajine.

2. Lamb, onions and almonds
This savoury lamb tajine is a classic in Marrakech.

3. Lamb and dates
Served at Le Tanjia (p73) and widely replicated in French cuisine.

4. Lamb and pear
Soft and tender, the pear is cooked so that it all but melts to the consistency of a purée.

5. Veal and green peas
The added saffron and ginger give this tajine a very special taste.

6. Lamb, prune and roast almonds
The sliced almonds add crunch to the sticky consistency of the prunes.

7. Veal and quince
Those who like a mixture of sweet and sour flavours should try this popular tajine.

8. Fish
Apart from at Dar Moha (p79), you will find the best, freshest fish tajines in Essaouira.

9. Lamb and artichokes
Strong-flavoured seasoned lamb works beautifully with caramelized onions and fresh artichokes.

10. Kefta tajine
These are small balls of spicy minced meat that are cooked slowly in a rich tomato sauce. An egg is occasionally added to the dish to make it even more flavourful.

GIFTS AND SOUVENIRS

1 Pottery
Almost every region of Morocco produces its own distinctive pottery; Marrakech style is notable for its use of the deep shade of majorelle blue. Local artisans shape their works using time-honoured techniques and rustic glazes. Pick up their fine wares at the stores of Sidi Ghanem *(p54)* for fixed prices.

2 Rugs
Marrakech's rugs were traditionally handwoven by Amazigh women in the Atlas Mountains. Today, these rugs are famous, and experts can identify exactly where a piece is from based on its style and colour. The best places to buy are in Souk des Tapis *(p27)*; when shopping for rugs, it's best to come with a rough price in mind.

3 Candles
Candles and tea light holders are used to sparkling effect in riads, bars and restaurants across the city. To take a little of Morocco's shimmering aesthetic home with you, look for them in the souks and boutiques of Guéliz and Sidi Ghanem *(p54)*. They are sold in so many variations, the challenge will be choosing the right one.

4 Jewellery
The local Amazigh jewellery is silver, chunky and heavy, though a number of artisans in Marrakech now produce more modern designs as well. In the silver shops of the souk, silver jewellery is usually priced according to its weight; reputable vendors will weigh items in front of you.

5 Metalworks
The streets around Souk des Ferronniers *(p27)* ring with the sound of hammer on metal, as artisans create ornate metal pieces. Discover decorative brassware at specialist ateliers throughout the souks, where hand-carved objects bearing floral patterns and calligraphic inscriptions are particular favourites.

6 Babouches
Babouches are Moroccan slippers, usually handmade from local leather (though imitations made of synthetic plastic are increasingly common). In their most traditional form, *babouches* are pointy toed and come in a variety of colours, without much decoration. Some boutiques and shops will customize *babouches* with a silk trim or sequins, or exquisitely carved designs.

7 Cactus Silk Cushions
Colourful stacks of these hand-woven and embroidered cushion covers line the souk streets. It's unclear if the yarn really is produced from the spiky leaves of the cactus plant, as many will tell you. They are, however, hand-spun, and the end result is a soft, silky and colourful cushion cover, with natural dyes such as saffron, indigo and henna used.

8 Fashion
Marrakech has inspired many fashionistas, so it's unsurprising that designers decide to open boutiques in the city. One great gift option is a

Colourful Moroccan pottery with traditional patterns

aftan, a traditional Moroccan dress, rich in heritage, that has evolved from palatial status into everyday wear. Caftans can be purchased in the souk, at designer boutiques in Mouassine (p78) and Guéliz (p84) or you can have one custom-made.

9 Leather Goods
Marrakech is known for its leather. Animal hides are treated by hand in the tanneries (p76) in the east of the Medina, and then dyed and shaped. Unsurprisingly, the shops of the souk are filled with leather goods, from purses and pouffes, to handbags and book bindings. Do plenty of window shopping before settling on an item.

10 Argan Oil
Argan oil is an almost mystical substance to which all kinds of properties are attributed. Part of its mystique can be credited to the rarity of argan trees, which only grow in southwest Morocco– meaning the pricing is heavily affected by low rainfall. The oil is sold all over the souks, quality oil has the consistency of olive oil and a neutral smell.

Argan oil extraction
in progress

TOP 10
MOROCCAN CARPETS

Hand-knotted Amazigh carpets

1. Handira
These creamy, sequined throws were traditionally worn by Amazigh brides as a wedding blanket.

2. Beni Ourain
The best-known of Moroccan rugs, these iconic carpets often feature black or brown motifs.

3. Boucherouite
Made using scraps of material, these rag rugs are bold and bright.

4. Zanafi
The city of Ouarzazate is home to these earth-toned, handcrafted rugs.

5. Azilal
These colourful wool rugs have geometric designs and bold colours on a neutral background.

6. Tuareg mats
Nomadic Tuareg tribesmen used these lightweight, durable mats as they withstand Saharan life.

7. Kilims
Characterized by deft and delicate weaving and embroidery, these thinner rugs are made of wool or silk.

8. Taznakht
There's a wide range of Taznakht rug styles, from simple to complex designs and neutral to bold colours.

9. Beni Mguild
Beni Mguild rugs are known for their natural indigo dyes that create deep shades of blue and purple.

10. Boujad
Featuring bright and vibrant colours, these rugs are patterned with traditional and modern art.

DAY TRIPS

2 Setti Fatma
🗺 C2

This small hidden village is a 90-minute drive to the south of the city. Here, at the head of the Ourika Valley in the foothills of the Atlas Mountains, visitors will find the starting point for a 15-minute stroll up to a fine waterfall and pool. Beyond this is a strenuous hike up a steep, rocky valley to six more waterfalls.

3 Essaouira
This medieval walled port-city (*p88*) on the Atlantic coast is only a few hours' drive from Marrakech. It has beaches, ramparts, souks, a fishing harbour and a fascinating hippy-era history.

4 Country Markets
Several small villages in the vicinity of Marrakech host weekly markets, with villagers from surrounding regions flocking to buy and sell produce, cheap clothing and assorted bric-a-brac. Cattle auctions are also common, as are makeshift salons of travelling barbers and dentists.

1 Imlil
🗺 C2

An hour-and-a-half drive from Marrakech, the mountain village of Imlil sits at the head of the Aït Mizane Valley in the High Atlas. Its altitude makes it a popular base for hiking. Most people come here to tackle nearby Jbel Toubkal (*p96*), but there are many other hikes of differing lengths and degrees of difficulty.

Skiers taking to the slopes
of the Oukaimeden

5 Oukaimeden
📍 C2

Snowfall on the Atlas between February and April means business for the ski resort at Oukaimeden, high above the Ourika Valley. There is a chairlift, and ski equipment can be hired on site. Reduced snowfall in recent years has, however, resulted in limited ski seasons for visitors.

6 Cascades d'Ouzoud
📍 D1 🏠 Riad Cascades d'Ouzoud
🌐 ouzoud.com

Two hours northeast on the Route de Fès, these are the most beautiful waterfalls in Morocco. Take a trek through wooded groves (*ouzoud* is Amazigh for olives) to reach the gorges of Oued El Abid. There is a lovely riad at the top of the cascades if you fancy spending the night.

7 Tameslouht
📍 C1

A 30-minute drive out of Marrakech on the Route d'Amizmiz, Tameslouht is a roadside village famed for its busy potters' cooperative. There are also weavers' workshops, an ancient mule-driven olive oil press and a crumbling kasbah. Start the trip with a visit to the Association Tameslouht – a useful information office on the main square, place Sour Souika, next to the main mosque. If the office is shut, one of the locals will be able to tell you where to find the potters.

8 Barrage Lalla Takerkoust
📍 C2 🏠 Le Flouha, BP 45 Barrage Lalla Taherkoust 🌐 leflouha-marrahech.com

Found to the south of Marrakech on the Route d'Amizmiz, this impressive artificial lake is backed by the beautiful Atlas Mountains. The clear water makes it a great place for a relaxing lakeside picnic. It is also popular with quad bikers. Try the local cuisine at one of the many waterside restaurants, including Le Flouka, which also offers accommodation.

9 Kasbah du Toubkal

A former tribal stronghold deep in the Atlas Mountains, this traditional kasbah is set at the foot of Jbel Toubkal (*p96*). The last part of the journey is done by mule. Visitors are brought up for an Amazigh lunch and hike, and are dropped back into town before dark. It is possible to stay overnight at the kasbah (*p116*).

10 Agafay Desert
📍 C3

The vast sandy plains of the Agafay Desert make for a perfect day trip from the city. Agafay Luxury Camp (*agafaydesertluxurycamp.com*) has stylish desert retreats and offers skydiving and hot-air balloon rides.

**Stunning natural beauty
of the Cascades d'Ouzoud**

AREA BY AREA

Dyed silk threads hanging in a souk

JEMAA EL-FNA AND THE KASBAH

The spiritual and historical heart of Marrakech, the Jemaa el-Fna (pronounced as a rushed "j'maf na"), was laid out as a parade ground by the founders of the city. Marrakech's next rulers constructed a walled royal domain to the south – known as the Kasbah – and the open ground passed into the public domain. Sultans and royal palaces have come and gone, but the Jemaa el-Fna remains eternally vital and has long been the centre for commerce in Marrakech. From sunset on, the life and bustle on the square reaches its peak as it fills with food stalls, storytellers, dancers and traditional Gnawa musicians.

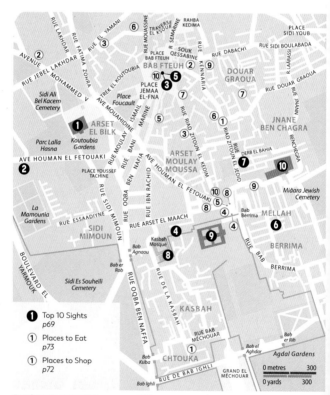

1 Top 10 Sights
p69

1 Places to Eat
p73

1 Places to Shop
p72

For places to stay in this area, see p114

Striking minaret of Koutoubia Mosque

1 Koutoubia Mosque

The Koutoubia Mosque *(p28)* is easily identified by its magnificent minaret (tower). This beautiful structure reaches a towering height of 77 m (252 ft), its rose-pink colour making for an eye-catching contrast, silhouetted against the cobalt blue of the sky by day and the fiery orange of twilight in the early evening. Although only Muslims are permitted inside the mosque, one of the doors on the east wall is often open, so visitors can peer through for a view.

2 La Mamounia Hotel

This former palace has been one of Marrakech's landmark hotels *(p40)* since it opened in 1923. While it has a reputation for hosting celebrities and visitors such as Winston Churchill, you don't have to be a guest to enjoy its poolside bar and restaurant – just dress the part.

3 Jemaa el-Fna

One of the most spectacular squares in North Africa, Jemaa el-Fna *(p22)* throngs with entertainers and locals as well as enthralled visitors from all over the world. Running south off Jemma el-Fna, Rue de Bab Agnaou is the Medina's pedestrianized "modern" main street, where you can find ATMs, internet cafés and pharmacies. Its narrow side alleys are home to good-value hotels.

4 Monde des Arts de la Parure

K4 40 Ksibat Nhass 10am–5pm Tue–Sun emapmarrakech.com

The Monde des Arts de la Parure, more commonly known as MAP, displays nearly 3,000 pieces of art, jewellery and other ethnographic treasures from more than 50 countries. The stunning collection was put together from pieces collected by ethnographic researchers Marlène and Paolo Ponce-Gallone over several decades of travel.

5 The Night Market

Evening brings a change to Jemaa el-Fna as the nightly food market *(p24)* takes over the square. Nearby is the rue Riad Zitoun el Jedid, which connects several major sights with Jemaa el-Fna, including the Dar Si Saïd Museum. Rue Riad Zitoun el Kedim links Jemaa el-Fna with the palace quarter.

Moorish-style room interior at the La Mamounia Hotel

6 The Mellah
📍 L5

The old Jewish quarter lies immediately east of the Kasbah. Visitors can enter via the Souk El Bab Salaam, a busy, covered market street across from a rose-planted square. The street leads to place Souweka and to the north you'll find one of the city's last working synagogues. Most of Marrakech's Jewish population left for Israel after World War II, in the 1950s and 1960s, but the number of graves in the nearby Miâara Jewish cemetery is testament to how many once lived here.

7 Musée Tiskiwin
📍 K4 🏠 Derb El Bahia, off rue Riad Zitoun El Jedid 📞 0524 38 91 92 🕐 9am–12:30pm & 2:30–6pm daily ♿

Located en route to the Monde des Arts de la Parure, this private house belongs to the Dutch anthropologist Bert Flint. An avid documenter of tribal arts and crafts, Flint amassed a fascinating and vast collection. Presented in his home for public viewing, the exhibition has been organized geographically as a journey that traces the old desert trade routes all the way from Marrakech to Timbuktu. Exhibit labels are in French, but there is an English guidebook.

8 Saadian Tombs
📍 J6 🏠 Rue de la Kasbah, Medina 🕐 9am–2:30pm daily 🌐 saadiantombs.com ♿

The historic Saadian tombs are located down a narrow alley that runs beside the Kasbah Mosque, which itself is just inside the beautiful and equally historic Bab Agnaou (p31). The small garden site is the resting place for some 66 royals of the Saadian dynasty, whose reign marked a golden era in the history of the city. This site can get easily crowded. Visit early morning or late afternoon for the best chance of avoiding the rush.

9 El Badi Palace

It is difficult to reconcile these ruins (p36) with a palace once reputed to be among the world's finest. An expanse of dusty ground within half-eroded walls, it retains some of its original elements, including sunken gardens and Moorish craftsmanship.

Traditional Amazigh clothing at Musée Tiskiwin

Exquisite mosaics and arches in the Saadian Tombs

10 Bahia Palace
Built in the 1890s by a powerful grand vizier (high official), the Bahia *(p32)* is an impressive minor palace complex approached by a long garden driveway. Inside, arrows direct visitors through a succession of large courtyards and private rooms that were used by the vizier and his four wives. All of the rooms are lavishly decorated with *zellij* tiling *(p45)*, sculpted stucco and carved cedarwood. The ruling sultan, Abdel Aziz, was so jealous of the riches of the Bahia that on the vizier's death he had parts of the palace stripped.

THE KING AND HIS PALACES

Throughout Moroccan history, the royal court has shifted base between Marrakech, Fès, Meknès and Rabat. The Almohads constructed Marrakech's first royal palace in the 12th century to the south of Jemaa el-Fna and it has been there ever since. The present King Mohammed VI had a smaller palace built for his personal use, outside the Bab Agnaou.

TO THE PALACES

Morning
Start on **Jemaa el-Fna** *(p22)*. On the southern side is an arch that leads to rue Riad Zitoun El Kedim. This area is mainly inhabited by locals and there is a distinct absence of souvenir vendors. At the southern end of the street, several places sell items that are fashioned out of old car tyres.

Across the main road is the **Marché du Mellah** *(p72)*, a market that's worth a quick look. Just southeast is the **place des Ferblantiers** *(p72)*, a paved plaza surrounded by metalworkers that leads through to the haunting **El Badi Palace**. After visiting the ruins, grab a snack from one of the stalls on the northwest corner of place des Ferblantiers.

Afternoon
Wander through the **Souk El Bab Salaam** *(p72)* before heading back north up the **rue Riad Zitoun El Jedid**. At the end of the street, on the right, is the gateway to the **Bahia Palace**, but anyone pushed for time should instead turn right and take the first left to the excellent **Monde des Arts de la Parure**. Just south is the equally interesting **Musée Tiskiwin**. Return to rue Riad Zitoun El Jedid and continue north where you will eventually reach **La Famille** *(p79)*, a tranquil spot where you can pause to have refreshing mint tea. Bear to the left to re-emerge onto the lively Jemaa el-Fna.

Moroccan handicrafts at Ensemble Artisanal Marrakech

Places to Shop

1. Rue Riad Zitoun El Jedid
📍K4
This street is lined with small, interesting boutiques. It is a pleasant alternative to the souks.

2. Ensemble Artisanal Marrakech
📍H3 🏠Ave Mohammed V
This government-run shop is a short walk from Jemaa el-Fna. You'll find traditional Moroccan handicrafts at fixed prices here, so no haggling.

3. RAQAS
📍J3 🏠1 rue el Ksour
Stylish Moroccan clothing is on offer at the store of this fair-trade fashion brand. Custom tailoring is available and there are accessories for sale too.

4. Place des Ferblantiers
📍K5
As an alternative to the souks, this is the place to go to for unique brass and iron lanterns that come in all shapes and sizes.

5. Aya's
📍K5 🏠11 bis, derb Jdid, Bab Mellah
🌐ayasmarrakech.com
It may be hard to find (a door away from Le Tanjia restaurant), but this boutique is worth seeking out for high-quality, traditional Moroccan clothing, silk, linen, jewellery and a wide range of accessories.

6. AlNour
📍J3 🏠Derb Moulay El Ghali 19
🌐alnour-textiles.com/shop
This social enterprise boutique features exquisite accessories and beautiful hand-embroidered clothing made with natural fibres, crafted by local women.

7. Le Cadeau Berbère
📍J3 🏠51 Jemaa el-Fna
📞0524 44 29 07
Established in 1930, this family-run textile specialist has an international clientele that includes interior designers, hoteliers and collectors.

8. Marché du Mellah
📍K5 🏠Ave Houman El Fetouaki 📅Fri
This indoor market sells flowers, household goods and local produce.

9. Atelier El Bahia
📍K5 🏠Rue Bahia Bab Mellah
📞0524 38 52 86
Even if you're not in the market for a new rug, you can still browse handmade shawls, throws and soft furnishings.

10. Souk El Bab Salaam
📍K5
Follow the distinct aromas wafting from the narrow alleys at the edge of the old Jewish quarter to this small and colourful herb and spice market in Place des Ferblantiers.

Places to Eat

Café Clock
K7 · 224 derb Chtouha, Kasbah · 9am–10pm daily · cafeclock.com · (Dh)

Serving camel burgers, almond milkshakes, homemade ice cream and all-day Amazigh breakfasts.

2. Le Marrakchi
K3 · 52 rue des Banques · 0524 44 33 77 · Noon–midnight daily · (Dh)(Dh)(Dh)

This restaurant has a lively roof terrace, with music and belly dancing.

3. Marrakech Henna Art Café
K4 · 35 derb Sqaya, Riad Zeitoun Lakdim · 11am–8:30pm daily · marrakechhennaartcafe.com · (Dh)

Moroccan dishes, including vegetarian and vegan options, are served here. Organic henna application available.

4. Kosybar
K5 · 47 place des Ferblantiers · 11:30am–1am daily · hosybar.com · (Dh)(Dh)(Dh)

Eat delicious Japanese-Mediterranean fusion dishes on the lovely, cool terrace or in the elegant interior of this restaurant.

5. Pâtisserie des Princes
J4 · Passage Prince Moulay Rachid · 7am–11pm daily · patisserie desprinces.com · (Dh)

A local version of a French pastry parlour, this place also offers ice creams, juices, tea and coffee.

6. Naranj
K4 · 84 rue Riad Zitoun el Jdid · Noon–10pm Mon–Sat · naranj. ma · (Dh)(Dh)

Take a break from tajines at this beautiful Lebanese spot serving flavourful dishes.

7. Pepe Nero
K4 · 17 derb Cherkaoui, Douar Graoua · 0524 38 90 67 · 7:30–11:30pm Tue–Sun · (Dh)(Dh)(Dh)

Excellent high-end Italian-Moroccan restaurant, worth splashing out on.

8. Le Tanjia
K5 · 14 derb Jedid, Hay Essalam, Mellah · Noon–midnight daily · tanjiaoriental.com · (Dh)(Dh)(Dh)

A three-floored temple of fine dining and entertainment with an excellent Moroccan menu and belly dancers.

9. Roti d'Or
K3 · 17 rue Kennaria, Medina · 0627 13 11 37 · Noon–4pm & 6–8:30pm Sat–Thu · (Dh)

A small but hip pavement café, Roti d'Or offers a wide range of burgers, french tacos and wraps that are prepared with a Moroccan twist.

10. Jemaa el-Fna
For the ultimate dining experience, try one of the stalls in the square (p22).

Fabulous poolside dining area at Pepe Nero

THE SOUKS

North of Jemaa el-Fna is a vast, tightly squeezed shopping area with dozens of narrow alleyways. These passageways are lined with shops the size of cupboards selling cloth, leather, metalwork, brass lanterns, carpets and jewellery. Historically, locals relied on these open-air markets for all their daily provisions, as the souks saw travelling merchants from all over the world regularly passing through them. With its strategic position at the very heart of Morocco, Marrakech welcomed the arrival of a dizzying array of goods, from culinary essentials to decorative textiles. Each area is dedicated to a single item, so a street may be packed with sellers of nothing but canary-yellow leather slippers, while another is filled with vendors of glazed pottery. A trip to the souks is an endurance test of just how long you can keep your money in your pocket. Come prepared to bargain, it's part of how the souk economy works.

1 Mouassine Fountain

J2

There are two main routes into the souks: rue Mouassine and rue Semmarine. The former runs past the Mouassine Mosque, after which the neighbourhood is named. A right turn at the mosque leads to a small plaza that holds a fountain with four bays – three for animals and one for humans. An arched gateway next to the fountain leads to the Souk des Teinturiers.

2 Dar Cherifa

J2 · 8 derb Charfa Lakhbir, Mouassine · 10am–midnight Thu–Tue, 10am–7pm Wed
w dar-cherifa.com

This beautifully renovated townhouse can be located by following the signs on the alley opposite the Mouassine Mosque. Featuring exquisite woodwork and carved plasterwork, some of the interiors date back to the 16th century. The house operates as a cultural centre with a performance space and work-shop. There's also a restaurant and *salon de thé* (tearoom).

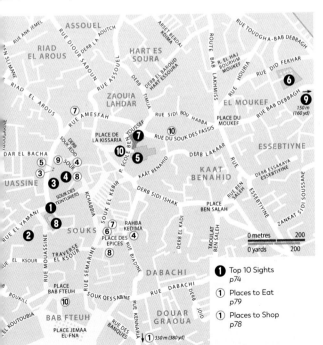

3 Fondouks
J2 192 rue Mouassine

To the north of the Mouassine Mosque, past Café Arabe (p79), is an excellent example of a *fondouk* – an old merchants' hostel. The rooms on the ground floor are used as workshops and the ones upstairs are mainly used for storage. This particular *fondouk* had a brush with stardom when it featured in the 1998 film *Hideous Kinky*, as the hotel where actress Kate Winslet and her daughters are shown to be staying.

4 Souk des Teinturiers
J2

The Dyers' Souk is a tangle of narrow alleyways east of the Mouassine Mosque. It becomes a riot of colours when hanks of just-dyed wools are hung out to dry. The dyers themselves are easy to spot; they are the men with bright red, purple and blue colours up to their elbows.

Dyers' workshops in the Souk des Teinturiers

1 Top 10 Sights p74
1 Places to Eat p79
1 Places to Shop p78

For places to stay in this area, see p114

5 Marrakech Museum

K2 Place Ben Youssef
0524 44 18 93 9am–6pm
daily Religious hols

This splendid 19th-century palace houses the Fondation Omar Benjelloun, which features ethnological and archaeological material as well as a wide-ranging collection of ancient and contemporary artwork. The former *hammam* makes an unusual exhibition space. Books, tea, coffee and pastries are also sold here.

6 The Tanneries

L1

A strong stomach is required to visit this particular quarter of the Medina. This is where animal hides are turned into leather. The work is done by hand as the hides are soaked in open vats. They look like a paintbox of watercolours from a distance, but up close smell so foul that guides give visitors sprigs of mint to hold under their noses. If you venture this far, pay a visit to the nearby Bab Debbagh (p31).

7 Ben Youssef Medersa

Located north of the Marrakech Museum, this beautiful building (p34) is an important centre of learning. A 16th-century theological college, it has tiny, window-less cells designed to house several hundred students. The central courtyard, which combines beautiful polychromic tiling, decorative plasterwork and detailed wood panelling to sublime effect, is its most stunning feature.

8 Mouassine Museum of Music

J2 4–5 derb el Hammam, Mouassine 9:30am–7pm daily
museedemouassine.com

A remarkable discovery was unearthed at this otherwise modest first-floor apartment. Hidden beneath the plaster were extraordinary painted ceilings and panels. It emerged that this had been the residence of a Saadian noble and below the later accretions, its 16th-century architecture remained intact. Visitors can view the ongoing restoration work and enjoy a cup of tea in the rooftop café.

PRETTY IN PINK

Every building in the Medina is painted pink. Why? It's the law, introduced during the era of French rule. The colour is actually ochre, the colour of the earth from which bricks were made in the past. Modern buildings still uphold this pink paint tradition, making the city a photographer's dream, particularly in the morning and evening light.

...handelier in the courtyard
...the Marrakech Museum

9 City Walls and Gates

The city walls and gates *(p30)*, ...uilt around the 1120s, surround the ...edina. While Bab Agnaou city gate, ...hich is located to the west of the ...aadian Tombs, is considered to be ...e most beautiful, Bab Debbagh gate ...ives you access to the tanneries. ...he internal staircase at Bab Debbagh ...eads to a roof from which you can ...njoy stunning, panoramic views of ...he city.

10 Almoravid Koubba

◻ K2 ◻ Place Ben Youssef ◻ 0524 44 18 93 ◻ 8:30am–6pm ...on–Fri ◻

...his fully intact building from the ...2th century is the only remaining ...xample of Almoravid architecture ...n the city, making it most likely the ...ldest building in Marrakech. Built ...y the Almoravid dynasty, it is assumed ...o be the ablutions area for the ...en Youssef Medersa. Its intricate ...ointed arches are reminiscent of ...he mosques of Andalucía, from the ...me of the Caliphate.

...Brick-built dome of the
Almoravid Koubba

HIDDEN MARRAKECH

Morning

Wrong turns and too many distractions make it impossible to plan a walk through the souks, which you should explore independently. On another day, head up rue Mouassine and take a left opposite the Mouassine Mosque before taking the first right to **Dar Cherifa** *(p47)*. Return to rue Mouassine and turn left at the T-junction. Take the first right through a low archway; follow the alley left and then right to No 22 and ring the bell for the eccentric **Ministero del Gusto** *(by appointment only; 0524 42 64 55)*, a gallery and concept store. Back on the main street, take a left towards the **Mouassine Fountain** *(p74)* or detour for a look at the **Musée Douiria de Mousassine**. Head north up rue Mouassine and stop at the **Café Arabe** *(p79)* for lunch.

Afternoon

After the café is the **Fondouk** *(p75)* made famous in *Hideous Kinky* starring Kate Winslet. Bear left onto rue Dar El Bacha, named for the Dar El Bacha palace, which has been converted into the **Dar El Bacha Museum**. It features temporary exhibitions devoted to Islamic art, science and knowledge. Continue past the Bab Doukkala Mosque, through a street market to the **Bab Doukkala gate** *(p30)* and exit the Medina; you could walk on to Guéliz or catch a taxi back to Jemaa el-Fna.

Places to Shop

Browsing rugs and carpets at Mustapha Blaoui

1. Mustapha Blaoui
📍 H2 🏠 142 rue Bab Doukkala
🌐 maisonblaoui.ma/welcome
Monsieur Blaoui's warehouse of Moroccan goods has everything from candleholders to wardrobes.

2. Ensemble Artisanal
📍 H3 🏠 Ave Mohammed V
📞 0524 44 35 03
A government store of Moroccan handicrafts. Though not as much fun as the souks, it is less stressful.

3. Kulchi
📍 J3 🏠 15 derb Nhhel 🌐 kulchi.com
A fashion-mag-friendly, Australian-owned business selling gorgeous carpets, hand-woven blankets, ceramics and other objects.

4. Michi
📍 J2 🏠 38 Souk el Kimakhin
Owned by a Japanese-Moroccan couple, this small shop has Moroccan homeware and artisanal goods with a Japanese style. The Moroccan slippers are particularly well made.

5. WAFL Design
📍 J2 🏠 202 rue Mouassine
A funky and innovative pop art concept store with bold styles and designs. Great for fun souvenirs and trendy T-shirts, colourful posters and home decor items.

6. Chabi Chic
📍 H2 🏠 91 rue Lalla Fatima Zahra
🌐 chabi-chic.com
Located within Nomad restaurant, this attractive boutique sells traditional and contemporary handmade pottery as well as beauty products.

7. Bazar du Sud
📍 K2 🏠 14 Souk des Tapis
🌐 bazardusud.com
Founded in 1940, Bazar du Sud is one of the oldest carpet manufacturers in Morocco. It has possibly the largest collection of handmade carpets and Amazigh textiles, backed up by an extremely professional sales service.

8. L'Art du Bain
📍 K3 🏠 13 Souk el Badine
🌐 artdubain.fr
This store deals in handmade soaps, from the traditional Moroccan *savon noir* to natural soaps infused with rose or musk.

9. Souk Cherifia
📍 J2 🏠 184 rue Mouassine, Medina
One of the best shopping stops for designer clothes, accessories and homeware, composed of more than 20 independent boutiques.

10. Beldi
📍 J3 🏠 9–11 rue Lahsour
📞 0524 44 10 76
This tiny boutique at the entrance to the souks showcases the work of brothers Toufik and Abdelhafid. They adapt Moroccan clothing for contemporary Western tastes to stunning effect.

Places to Eat

1. La Famille
K4 42 rue Riad Zitoun Jdid Noon–3:30pm Tue–Sun lafamillemarrakech.com · Dh

Enjoy Mediterranean cuisine in the shade of this tranquil garden restaurant.

2. La Maison Arabe
H2 1 derb Assehbé, Medina cenizaro.com/lamaisonarabe Dh Dh Dh

Moroccan cuisine in the main restaurant. French, Moroccan and Asian in Les Trois Saveurs.

3. Café Arabe
J2 184 rue Mouassine 10am–midnight daily cafearabe.com Dh Dh

Italian and Moroccan food is served on the pillow-strewn roof terrace.

4. L'mida
K2 78 bis derb Nhhel Rahba Kdima 0524 44 36 62 Noon–11pm daily · Dh

Enjoy modern twists on Moroccan dishes while admiring city views from the roof terrace.

5. Dar Moha
H2 81 rue Dar El Bacha Noon–3pm & 7:30–10pm daily darmoha.ma · Dh Dh Dh

Sit by the pool and enjoy the exceptional food at this spot.

Candlelit rooftop terrace at Le Foundouk

6. Café des Épices
K3 75 Rahba Lakdima 9am–11pm daily cafedesepices.ma · Dh

Calm and charming, this café offers a welcome break from the souks.

7. Atay Café
K2 62 rue Amesfah, Sidi Abdelaziz 0661 34 42 46 10am–10pm daily · Dh

A beautiful, friendly little café with three terraces. As well as Moroccan staples, it serves dishes like ravioli, salads and has a selection of juices.

8. Nomad
K3 1 derb Arjaan, off Rahba Kedima Noon–11pm daily nomadmarrakech.com · Dh Dh

Excellent contemporary restaurant owned by the same people behind Café des Épices and Terrasse des Épices above the Souk Cherifia.

9. Pikala Café
H2 139 Arset Aouzal 9am–5pm daily pikalabikes.com · Dh Dh

Pikala's healthy seasonal menu features breakfast bowls, refreshing salads and homemade fruit juices. It also offers a bike rental service, a co-working space, and a full schedule of live music events.

10. Le Foundouk
K2 55 rue du Souk des Fassis 7pm–midnight Thu–Tue foundouk.com · Dh Dh

Wonderfully stylish restaurant with a French-Moroccan menu. There's also a romantic roof terrace.

THE NEW CITY

It was only with the arrival of the French in the early 20th century that Marrakech broke out of the walls of the Medina. The new colonial rulers built their own *ville nouvelle* of broad avenues, villas and parks. Over time, Moroccans aspiring for a better lifestyle moved out into this new town, lured by serviceable plumbing, electricity and cars. Now known as Guéliz – from *église*, French for church (the area has the city's first) – the New City has plenty for tourists looking to explore Marrakech's modern facet. The streets are lined with fine restaurants, beautiful galleries, huge shopping plazas and small shops. In the evening, there's a vibrant nightlife scene with a great mix of bars and nightclubs here.

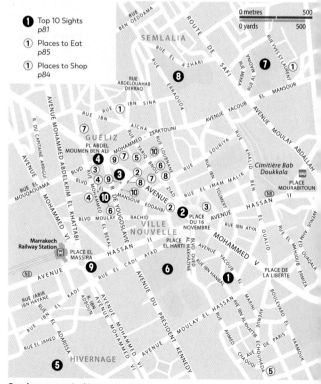

1 Top 10 Sights *p81*

1 Places to Eat *p85*

1 Places to Shop *p84*

For places to stay in this area, see p116

Altar at the Église des Saints-Martyrs de Marrakech

1 Église des Saints-Martyrs de Marrakech

C5 Rue El Imam Ali, Guéliz
For Services 6:30pm Mon–Sat, 10am Sun eglisemarrakech.org

Built in 1926, this Catholic church stands as a tribute to six 13th-century Franciscan friars beheaded by the sultan as a punishment for preaching Christianity. Its spartan interior is enlivened by colourful panels of stained glass. The church's bell tower is now overshadowed by the minaret of an adjacent mosque. Protestant services are held in the library on Sunday at 10:30am.

2 Avenue Mohammed V

C5

This wide avenue, named after Mohamed V, is the spine of Marrakech. It connects the old and new cities, running from the Koutoubia to Jbel Guéliz (Mount Guéliz). Along the way are three major roundabouts: place de la Liberté with its modern fountain; place du 16 Novembre where the main post office is located; and the heart of the New City, place Abdel Moumen Ben Ali.

3 Mauresque Architecture

The French brought with them European architectural styles, which mixed with local Moorish influences to create a new style, soon dubbed "Mauresque". Avenue Mohammed V is dotted with Mauresque structures, especially where it intersects with rue de la Liberté; here several buildings have clean Modernist lines but also pavement arcades to shade pedestrians from the sun.

4 Hotel La Renaissance

C5 89 Angle blvd Zerhtouni and Mohammed V, Guéliz renaissance-hotel-marrakech.com

Built in 1952, La Renaissance was the first hotel in the modern district of Guéliz, and has since become an iconic building in Marrakech. The rooftop terrace is the perfect spot to sample delicious cocktails and take in the splendour of the Koutoubia (p28) and the market at Jemaa el-Fna. It also offers a breathtaking panorama of the fashionable Guéliz area along with serene views of the Atlas Mountains. The hotel has a great outdoor swimming pool.

5 Hivernage
🅥 C6

South of Guéliz and immediately west of the Medina walls, Hivernage is a small neighbourhood of quiet streets that are shaded by trees. Its mix of villas and some five-star hotels ensures a tranquil atmosphere. There are one or two fairly good restaurants in the area, in addition to one of the city's favourite nightspots, Comptoir Darna (p85).

6 Jnane El Harti
🅥 C5

A small and pretty park just off place du 16 Novembre, Jnane El Harti was originally laid out by the French as a formal garden and zoo. Named after former owner El Harti, a wealthy Moroccan businessman, the park is a popular spot for visitors and locals alike. In a 1939 essay titled "Marrakech", George Orwell writes of feeding gazelles here. Numerous notices provide information about the various species of plants growing in the many flowerbeds. The plaza fronting the park gates is often used for events.

MOVIE TIME

The city has been a popular Hollywood film location since the 1950s and it continues to star in blockbusters, including *Sex and the City 2* (2010) and *Men in Black: International* (2019). Movie buffs and the rich and famous descend on Hivernage in December for the Marrakech International Film Festival. Special events are held across the city.

7 Jardin Majorelle

A 10-minute walk east of place Abdel Moumen Ben Ali, these utterly enchanting gardens (p38) are the absolute must-see sight in the New City. Created in the 1920s and 1930s by the French painter Jacques Majorelle, they were owned by famous French couturier and part-time Morocco resident Yves Saint Laurent until his death in 2008. Open to the public, the gardens feature botanical specimens from the far corners of the world. There's also a museum of Amazigh culture, a gift shop, gallery, café and a garden memorial to YSL. Next door is the Musée Yves Saint Laurent.

Tombstones in the burial grounds, European Cemetery

8 European Cemetery

🔲 C4 🔲 Rue Erraouda 🔲 Apr–Sep: 7am–7pm daily; Oct–Mar: 8am–6pm daily

North of boulevard Mohammed Zerktouni is a walled graveyard dating back to the 1920s. It is the burial ground of many of the original inhabitants of Guéliz. A dozen English Protestant missionaries also rest here. Most notable is the tomb of Kate Hosali, who founded SPANA, a charity for working animals of the world.

9 Théâtre Royal

🔲 B5 🔲 Ave Hassan II 🔲 0524 43 15 16 🔲 Hours vary, call ahead

This striking piece of architecture by leading local light, Charles Boccara, is crowned by a grand dome. The interior has a beautiful, tiled courtyard linking a 1,200-seat open-air theatre and an 800-seat opera house. The work of local artists and sculptors is occasionally displayed here.

10 Spanish Quarter

🔲 B5

Running west off rue de Yougoslavie is a narrow street lined with single-storey houses of a unique design. This shady lane, planted with mulberry trees, constitutes the city's old Spanish quarter, a testament to Marrakech's once considerable Hispanic population.

Towering cacti and palm trees at Jardin Majorelle

OLD CITY TO NEW CITY

Morning

Start next to the **Koutoubia Mosque** (*p28*) and head up **avenue Mohammed V** (*p81*). After a few minutes you will come to **Arsat Moulay Abdeslem** (*p51*) on the left, known as "Cyber Park" after its popular internet centre. Exit the Medina through the Bab Nkob, plunging into the large traffic island, place de la Liberté. Take the second left after the traffic junction, followed by the first right, and you'll find yourself in the historic **Église des Saints-Martyrs de Marrakech** (*p81*). Continue north up avenue Yacoub Marini to reach **Jnane El Harti** park. Cross the place du 16 Novembre to lunch at the **Grand Café de la Poste** (*p85*).

Afternoon

The road next to McDonald's leads to the **Marché Central** (*p84*) which is well worth the 15-minute detour. Return to Mohammed V for some of the best shopping in town. The next major traffic intersection, place Abdel Moumen Ben Ali, is overlooked by the Parisian-style **Café Les Négociants** (*p85*) which is a good place to rest your feet. You are now at the heart of Guéliz; in addition to shopping, there are several interesting galleries nearby (*p46*), as well as excellent eating and drinking options (*p85*).

Places to Shop

A range of homeware for sale at 33 Rue Majorelle

1. 33 Rue Majorelle

C4 33 rue Yves Saint-Laurent, Guéliz 33ruemajorelle.com

This popular concept store has clothes, accessories, jewellery and handicrafts made by local designers.

2. Place Vendôme

B5 141 ave Mohammed V 0524 43 52 63 9am–1pm & 3–7pm daily

The leather items here are of much greater quality than those sold in the souks and are designed with more of an international style and flavour.

3. Marché Central

C4 Rue Ibn Toumert

A variety of foodstuffs are available at this popular market, as well as traditional handicrafts.

4. Maison ARTC

B5 96 rue Mohammed el Beqa 11am–8pm Mon–Sat maison artc.com

Run by the visionary Moroccan-Israeli designer Artsi Ifrach, Maison ARTC stocks an eclectic range of clothing items, noted for their vibrant patterns and outlandish charm.

5. Moor

B5 7 rue des Vieux Marrakchis, Guéliz 0524 45 82 74 Sun

Sublime clothing and houseware, though it can be a little pricey.

6. Café du Livre

B5 44 rue Tarik Bnou Ziad 0524 44 69 21 Sun

A haven for book lovers, offering a range of titles from across the globe. It also has a café with Wi-Fi access and is a good spot for a drink or a quick lunch.

7. Galerie Birkemeyer

B5 169–171 rue Mohammed El Behal 8:30am–12:30pm & 3–7:30pm Mon–Sat, 9am–12:30pm Sun galerie-birkemeyer.com

Great for leather goods such as elegant jackets, handbags and trunks as well as international designer sportswear.

8. L'Orientaliste

B5 11 & 15 rue de la Liberté 0524 43 40 74 9am–12:30pm & 3–7:30pm Mon–Sat, 10am–12:30pm Sun

A small shop with interesting items such as tea glasses, jewellery and antique furniture. It is also known for its amazing perfumes.

9. Atika Chaussures

B5 34 rue de la Liberté, Guéliz Sun atika-marrakech.com

Shop for good-quality leather shoes, especially Moccasins and loafers in myriad colours at this fashionable store.

10. Scènes du Lin

B5 70 rue de la Liberté Sun scenesdelin.com

Browse through finely designed curtains with Fès embroidery and a selection of unusual lamps at this interior decor store. It also offers custom-made furniture and other home accessories.

Places to Eat

1. Amal

B4 · Rue Allal Ben Ahmed, Guéliz · 8:30am–12:30pm & noon–3:30pm daily · amalnonprofit.org · Dh

Dine in and support this non-profit organization for disadvantaged women. Cooking classes available.

2. Grand Café de la Poste

B5 · Cnr blvd El Mansour Eddahbi & ave Imam Malik · 8am–1am daily · grandcafedelaposte.restaurant · Dh Dh

The Art Deco interior of this café, built in 1925, is largely intact. The service can be patchy.

3. +61

B5 · 96 rue Mohammed el Beqal · Noon–4pm & 6–11pm Mon–Sat · plus61.com · Dh Dh

A cosy restaurant offering Moroccan fare, as well as pasta and pizza.

4. La Trattoria Marrakech

B5 · 179 rue Mohammed El Behal · Noon–3pm & 7pm–midnight daily · latrattoriamarrakech.com · Dh Dh

The city's best Italian restaurant is housed in a beautiful villa with seats beside the pool.

5. Comptoir Darna

C6 · Ave Echouhada · 7:30pm–1am daily · comptoirmarrakech.com · Dh Dh

A great venue for a night out, Comptoir Darna serves excellent North African cuisine with dishes such as seafood tajine and salmon steak, plus a few vegetarian options. Upstairs, there's also a chic lounge bar.

6. Sahbi Sahbi

B4 · 37 Boulevard Mansour Eddahbi, Guéliz · 7pm–1am Tue–Sun · sahbisahbi.com · Dh Dh Dh

Run entirely by women, this modern restaurant has a lovely open kitchen and is known for its creative dishes.

7. Al Fassia

B5 · 55 blvd Mohammed Zerhtouni · Noon–2:30pm & 7:30–11pm Wed–Mon · alfassia.com · Dh Dh

An excellent frill-free restaurant with a lovely, peaceful garden.

8. Le Catanzaro

B5 · 42 rue Tarih Bnou Ziad, Guéliz · Noon–2:30pm & 7:15–11pm Mon–Sat · catanzaro.ma · Dh

Reliable French/Italian restaurant serving pizzas, pastas and steaks.

9. Café Les Négociants

B5 · Cnr ave Mohammed V & blvd Mohammed Zerhtouni · 7am–11pm daily · cafelesnegociants.com · Dh

Stop at this popular café for a sip of strong, tar-like coffee.

10. MY Kechmara

B5 · 3 rue de la Liberté · 9am–midnight Mon–Sat, 9am–5pm Sun · myhechmara-rooftop.com · Dh Dh

This hip bar-restaurant wouldn't look out of place in Paris.

Stylish dining room interior at the MY Kechmara

ESSAOUIRA

Where Marrakech is a uniform pink, this sun-beaten town, two hours and 30 minutes away on Morocco's Atlantic coast, is a nautical blue and white. The city as we know it today was largely designed in the 1760s, when French architect Théodore Cornut remodelled Essaouira's infrastructure and its famous fortress. Its prosperity peaked in the 18th and 19th centuries, when it became a key point along the caravan route from sub-Saharan Africa to the Atlas Mountains and on to Marrakech, bringing traders from all over the region. It faded from consciousness in the 20th century, but drew plenty of travelling hippies and attracted the likes of Jimi Hendrix and Frank Zappa in the 1960s and early 1970s. Today, its agreeably languid atmosphere is stirred only in late afternoon when the fishing fleet returns. Essaouira is known as the "Windy City" because of the constant winds that blow from the sea.

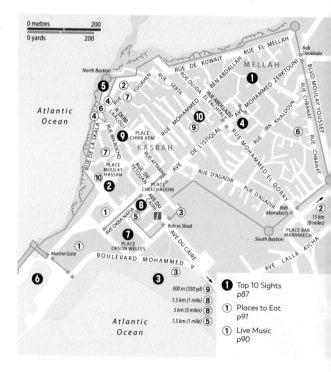

❶ Top 10 Sights
p87

① Places to Eat
p91

① Live Music
p90

Mellah
Q1

During the 18th and 19th centuries, the Jewish community gained prominence in Essaouira, becoming the most important economic group. The community has long since left and the town's Jewish quarter, or *mellah*, is in a dilapidated state. Visitors can reach it by following the alleys just inside the ramparts beyond Skala de la Ville. Former Jewish residences are fronted by balconies. In some cases, the Hebrew inscriptions on their lintels are also visible.

Moroccan handmade ceramic plate at a souk

2 Place Moulay Hassan
N2

Place Moulay Hassan is the focal point of Essaouira. A square in two parts, narrow and elongated to the north and opening out at the southern end, it lies between the Medina proper and the port, and everybody passes through it at some point. It is lined by small cafés where locals spend their time.

3 The Beach
P2

Essaouira's beach, to the south of the Medina, is one of the finest in Morocco. However, the strong winds that batter this part of the Atlantic coast can make it a little cold – not that this bothers the windsurfers or the boys who play football here.

4 The Souks
P1

At the heart of the Medina is a lively market, the Souk Jdid, divided into four quarters. There is a daily souk for fish, spice and grains, and a cloistered square, known as the Joutia, where second-hand items are sold.

5 Ramparts
N1

Essaouira's current layout can be traced back to 1765. That year, the town's local ruler captured a French ship and hired one of its passengers, who was an architect, to rebuild his port. He had the city surrounded with a heavy defensive wall, much of which still stands today. The most impressive stretch is the Skala de la Ville, where you can go for a walk along the top of the ramparts and examine several of the ancient cannons in the area.

Essaouira's ramparts as seen from the beach

Fishing boats moored in the port of Essaouira

6 The Port
N2

Guarded by a small square fortress, Essaouira's port, the Skala du Port, is still a working concern complete with a boat yard. Even today, vessels are constructed out of wood. A daily market kicks into life between 3pm and 5pm with the arrival of the day's catch. This port also supplies fresh fish to the local market and the town's many seafood restaurants. Visitors can watch as the fish are auctioned off and sample the fresh produce by indulging in the sardines that are grilled to order at the port end of place Moulay Hassan.

7 Place Orson Welles
N2–P2

Between the Medina walls and the beach is a small park-like square named place Orson Welles, in honour of the great film-maker who travelled to Essaouira in 1949 to shoot his version of *Othello*. Since then, Essaouira and the surrounding area have been used as movie locations in many international film projects, including Oliver Stone's epic *Alexander* and Ridley Scott's *Kingdom of Heaven*.

8 Galerie Damgaard
P2 Ave Ohba Bin Nafia, Medina 0524 78 44 46 9am–1pm & 3–7pm daily

For about a quarter of a century a generation of painters and sculptors have made Essaouira an important centre of artistic activity. Many of these artists were brought to public attention by Dane Frederic Damgaard, an antique dealer who used to run this influential gallery, until he retired in 2006. Along with a well-curated display of art, this private gallery is also a great place to shop for souvenirs and books on local art and culture.

Musée Sidi Mohamed Ben Abdellah

N1 Rue derb Laâlouj, Medina
0524 47 53 00 8:30am–6:30pm Wed–Mon

This small ethnographic museum occupies a 19th-century house that was formerly the town hall. Named after the founder of Essaouira, Mohammed Ben Abdellah, the museum features a collection of ancient crafts, weapons, carpets, jewellery and historical coins from the region. Also displayed here are the musical instruments and accessories that were used by religious brotherhoods . You can also view some stunning examples of traditional Amazigh and Jewish costumes here.

10 The Medina

P1

As in Marrakech, Essaouira's Medina is a labyrinth of narrow streets. However, it is not as hard to navigate as it is bisected by one long, straight street. This street begins at the port and runs all the way up to the north gate, the Bab Doukkala, undergoing two name changes along the way.

The Medina's narrow alley lined with shops

A DAY BY THE SEA

Morning

It is possible to do Essaouira as a day trip from Marrakech. You can get an early morning **CTM** bus (p108), a Supratours coach (p108) at 7:45am or a grand taxi from a rank behind the bus station and arrive by 10am or 11am. You will probably enter the city from the Bab Marrakech and follow rue Mohammed El Qorry to the main crossroads of the Medina, which is also the middle of the **souks** (p26). Walk south down avenue de L'Istiqlal, taking a right turn into shop-lined rue Attarine. The first left leads down to **place Moulay Hassan** (p87), a great place for a drink at one of the many cafés such as Café Bachir.

Afternoon

From the port, backtrack to place Moulay Hassan but take a left at the famed **Taros** café (p90) and follow the narrow alley, rue de la Skala, along the inside of the high sea wall. There are some woodcarving workshops here. After a short walk, head up to the **ramparts** (p87) for a wonderful view. Descend and then continue to mellah (p87). Find your way back to the souks and again head along avenue de L'Istiqlal south. Take a left on avenue du Caire, exiting by the Bab Es Sbaâ and taking a right for the **beach** (p87). **Le Chalet de la Plage** (p91) is perfect for dinner by the ocean.

Live Music

1. Gnaoua World Music Festival
⊠ N2 ⌂ Place Moulay Hassan (main stage) ⓦ festival-gnaoua.net
Held every year in June, this festival is the city's largest cultural event celebrating African music and the distinctive Gwana style.

2. Il Mare
⊠ P1 ⌂ Rue Yemen 43 ⓦ ilmares saouira.com
Open for dinner and drinks, Il Mare is one of the city's finest spots to catch local live music, seven nights a week.

3. D'Jazy Essaouira
⊠ P2 ⌂ Complexe Commercial Bin Al Aswar ⓒ 0607 17 60 12 ⊙ Tue–Sat
This hip fusion jazz club offers live music from 9pm onwards. The bar snacks and cocktails are excellent.

4. Salut Maroc
⊠ N1 ⌂ 32 rue Ibn Rochd ⓦ salutmaroc.com
The rooftop of this hotel comes to life at night with regular live music sessions by local musicians.

5. Beach and Friends
⊠ P3 ⌂ Ave Mohammed V ⓒ 0524 47 45 58
This beach bar offers great tapas and relaxed live music through the afternoon and evening.

6. Ocean Vagabond
⊠ P3 ⌂ 4 blvd Lalla Aichaangle ⓒ 0524 47 42 85
Enjoy a casual dinner with live music played by DJs or local musicians.

7. Taros
⊠ N2 ⌂ Place Moulay Hassan ⓒ 0524 47 64 07
Situated on the edge of the Medina, this café hosts guest DJs on its rooftop terrace, each spinning a mix of beats from around the world.

8. So Lounge
⊠ F3 ⌂ Domaine Mogador, Diabat ⓦ sofitel.accor.com
Located in the Sofitel Marrakech's lush gardens, this excellent nightclub has resident and international DJs playing the latest hits.

9. Mega Loft
⊠ P2 ⌂ 35 ave de l'Istiqlal ⓒ 0613 98 19 87
Every night, DJs play a mix of international and Moroccan music at this popular club.

10. Place Moulay Hassan
⊠ N2
Essaouira's central square comes alive in the evening when Gnawa musicians play the *gimbri*, a three-stringed lute-like instrument that produces hypnotic sounds.

Celebrating the Gnaoua World Music Festival, Essaouira

Places to Eat

1. Port-Side Fish Stalls

📍 N2 🏠 Place Moulay Hassan · Dh

The best meal in Essaouira is seafood fresh off the boat, grilled and eaten at a group of stalls on the port side of place Moulay Hassan.

2. La Fromagerie

📍 A1 🏠 Douar Larabe, Route Côtière de Safi 📞 0666 23 35 34 🕐 Noon–midnight daily · Dh Dh

Located just a ten-minute taxi ride from the Medina, La Fromagerie is a small hillside restaurant. Each dish offered here involves cheese and is made on the premises.

3. Le Chalet de la Plage

📍 P3 🏠 Blvd Mohammed V 📞 0524 47 59 72 🕐 Noon–2:30pm & 6:30–10:30pm · Dh Dh

Enjoy the superb beachfront setting that matches the quality of fresh fish and seafood at Le Chalet de la Plage.

4. Les Alizés Mogador

📍 N1 🏠 26 rue de la Skala 📞 0524 47 68 19 🕐 Noon–3:30pm & 7:30–11pm daily · Dh

This restaurant serves hearty portions of Moroccan food.

5. La Table Madada

📍 P2 🏠 Rue Youssef El Fassi 📞 0524 47 21 06 🕐 7–10pm Wed–Mon · Dh Dh

The Madada riad is one of the cosiest spots in town. The contemporary Moroccan menu focuses on fresh fish and Atlantic seafood alongside produce from the market.

Outdoor seating on the terrace at Taros

6. Umia

📍 N2 🏠 22 rue de la Skala 📞 0524 78 33 95 🕐 7pm–midnight Wed–Mon · Dh Dh

Sample lobster ravioli and chocolate fondant at this French restaurant.

7. Triskala Café

📍 N1 🏠 Rue Touahen 📞 0643 40 55 49 🕐 12:30–3:30pm & 6:30–10pm daily · Dh

A daily-changing menu of fresh fish, vegetarian and vegan dishes served in cave-like rooms just inside the city's seafront ramparts.

8. Zahra's Grill

📍 N2 🏠 Rue Amira Lalla Meriem 📞 0661 90 57 22 🕐 1–3pm & 7–9:30pm daily 🕐 Mid-Nov–mid-Mar · Dh Dh

Expect fabulous seafood, from the octopus salad to the lobster risotto.

9. Côté Plage

📍 Q3 🏠 Blvd Mohammed V 📞 0524 47 90 00 · Dh Dh Dh

Part of the MBeach Sofitel complex, this beachfront café serves tapas and flavoursome barbecued meats.

10. Taros

📍 N2 🏠 Place Moulay Hassan 📞 0524 47 64 07 🕐 10am–midnight Mon–Sat · Dh Dh

Enjoy the mix of Moroccan and French dishes at Taros. There is live music here most nights.

A street in Essaouira's Medina

TIZI-N-TEST PASS

The high-altitude Tizi-n-Test Pass, the more westerly of the two great passes over the Atlas Mountains, is cautiously navigated by the R203 highway to Taroudant. Although the distance between the two cities is only 223 km (138 miles), the road's tortuous hairpins demand so much respect from drivers that the journey takes nearly five hours – not including time to stop off and take in the views along the way. The highway heading through the summit is a remarkable piece of engineering. It was constructed by French colonialists between 1926 and 1932, and was the first modern road to link Marrakech to the Souss plains and the Atlas Mountains to the wider Sahara. Travellers without their own vehicle or *grand taxi* can make the trip by public transport: southbound buses depart Marrakech each morning. From November to April, the pass is sometimes blocked by snow.

1 Top 10 Sights
p95

1 Beyond the Pass
p98

For places to stay in this area, see p116

Scenic Tizi-n-Test Pass in the High Atlas mountains

1 Tizi-n-Test Pass
🗺 B2

How much travellers enjoy the experience of this 2,092-m (6,861-ft) pass depends on whether they are a passenger or in the driver's seat. Drivers have to keep their eyes glued to the road ahead in order to negotiate the endless hairpin bends. The narrow road, with no safety barriers, means there aren't many opportunities to enjoy the beautiful views. But for those in the passenger seat, the vistas across the plains of the Souss to the south are spectacular.

2 Ouirgane
🗺 C2

A pretty little village 16 km (10 miles) south of Asni, Ouirgane is hidden among the tree-lined valley above the Oued Nifis river. Here, there is a shrine to a Jewish saint as well as two salt factories (one modern, one traditional). The village is a great base for hiking, though the significant damage caused by the 2023 earthquake (p96) is still visible here.

3 Asni
🗺 C2

The village of Asni lies at a fork in the road – a left turn leads up to the village of Imlil and the striking kasbahs of Tamadot (p117) and Toubkal (p116).

Jbel Toubkal dominates the view to the west, but there is little to explore at Asni itself, apart from shops selling trinkets (although these are cheaper in Marrakech). The highlight here is the country market held on Saturdays – one of the largest in the Atlas Mountains.

4 Taroudant
🗺 B2

Built on the proceeds of gold brought from the Sahara, Taroudant was the capital of the Saadian dynasty in the early 16th century. Today, enclosed within reddish-yellow walls, the city resembles a smaller version of Marrakech. It features a grand kasbah, as well as some tanneries. You will also find two excellent souks in Taroudant.

Wide range of items at a souk in Taroudant

5 Tahanoute
🔘 C1

The administrative centre of Tahanoute is just a 20-minute drive south of Marrakech. The old village has a cascade of red clay houses that surround a massive rock sheltering the shrine of Sidi Mohammed El Kebir, whose festival is celebrated at Mouloud – the birthday of the Prophet Mohammed. This was the subject of Winston Churchill's last painting in 1958. A market is held here every Tuesday.

6 Moulay Brahim
🔘 C2

South of Tahanoute, the road winds uphill to Moulay Brahim, named after a local saint. There is a green-roofed shrine dedicated to him in the middle of the village which non-Muslims are forbidden to enter.

7 Jbel Toubkal
🔘 C2

Take the left fork at Asni to Imlil (*p64*) at the foot of Jbel Toubkal, North Africa's highest peak. Climbing Toubkal is not particularly difficult, but the fact that it is a high-altitude hike over rough terrain should be taken into account. Mountain guides can be hired in the centre of Imlil at the

SEPTEMBER 2023 EARTHQUAKE

In September 2023, a devastating earthquake damaged this area of the High Atlas, in some cases irreparably. Extensive renovations are ongoing, and a gradual reopening of areas and sights across the region is expected. Check for up-to-date information on closures before visiting.

bureau des guides (*0524 48 56 26*). The Kasbah du Toubkal (*p116*), just up the hill, is a good place to stay.

8 Lalla Takerkoust
🔘 C2

The town of Lalla Takerkoust is famous for its large artificial lake and sweeping views of the Atlas Mountains. The area around the town blooms with an abundance of flora during the harvest season, as Saharan nomads planted flowers here in the early 18th century, but the town's charms extend beyond its beauty. There are many hiking trails

leading out to the country, and canoeing is a popular activity too. The area also has several hotels and restaurants.

9 Kasbah Talaat-n-Yacoub
🔲 C2

South of Ouirgane, the road climbs steadily through a bare and rocky landscape. After you pass through the Amazigh hamlet of Ijoujak, the hilltop fortress of Kasbah Talaat-n-Yacoub is visible to the right. This was once a stronghold of the Goundafi tribe who controlled access to the Tizi-n-Test pass until the early 20th century, when they were subdued by the French.

10 Tichka Plateau
🔲 B2

Set among beautiful meadows, the Tichka Plateau is found to the north of Taroudant. Particularly striking in spring, it is a fine place to go trekking, but is best enjoyed with qualified guides. Go to the *bureau des guides* in Imlil (p64) to arrange a guided trek.

Mountaineer climbing snow-clad Jbel Toubkal

A DAY IN TAROUDANT

Morning
Although **Taroudant** (p95) resembles a more ramshackle Marrakech at first sight, it has more of an African identity than an Arab one. Begin your exploration on place El Alaouyine, known by its Amazigh name of place Assarag. Walk down boulevard Mohammed V and head east into Souk Arabe, famed for its antique shops. At the souk's edge, **Boulangerie El Widad** (+212 5288 52150) on boulevard Mohammed V, offers tasty Moroccan pastries. South of the main street and across place El Nasr is Souk Berbère, the main fruit and vegetable market. Return north up Avenue Bir Anzarené and take a right; sample the tajines at **Chez Nada** (15 ave Moulay Rachid).

Afternoon
As you walk east on avenue Moulay Rachid along a path lined with orange trees, you will come upon the triple-arched Saadian Gates at Bab El Kasbah. These lead to the walled kasbah quarter built by Mohammed ech-Cheikh, who made it the capital of the Saadian empire. The poorest part of town, it used to house the governor's palace. Stop for a snack at one of the local cafés and then make your way back to the Bab El Kasbah. Hop into a taxi and head back to place El Alaouyine.

Beyond the Pass

1. Taznakht
C2

About 85 km (53 miles) east of Taliouine, beneath Jbel Siroua, lies Taznakht. This town is famed for its carpets woven by the Ouaouzgite tribe. Each carpet is handcrafted and features a unique design. Here, visitors can also learn about various weaving techniques.

2. The Atlas Mountains
B2

The Atlas Mountains range in a diagonal right across Morocco. To the north are the low-rise Middle Atlas, covered with Aleppo pine and Atlas cedar. Further south are the soaring peaks of the High Atlas, including the 3,555-m-(11,667-ft-) high Jbel Aoulime, which can be reached by a road north of Taroudant.

3. Taliouine
C2

Taliouine, a town between two mountain chains, is home to a stately kasbah once owned by the Glaoui.

Though dilapidated, it is still inhabited. The town is also one of the world's biggest saffron-growing areas.

4. The Anti-Atlas
C3

As the R106 from Taliouine crosses the Anti-Atlas at the 94-km (58-mile) mark, you'll find Igherm, a large mountain village where women wear black with coloured headbands. The village is the base of the Ida Oukensous tribe, who are renowned for making daggers and guns. The houses are built of pink stone, with their windows outlined in blue.

5. Tioute Kasbah
B3

About 37 km (23 miles) southeast of Taroudant, the imposing Tioute Kasbah (containing a restaurant) dominates the palm groves. This was the location for the 1954 film *Ali Baba and the Forty Thieves*. It is also the perfect spot for a picnic with a view. Nearby, on the banks of Wadi Souss, which attracts many migratory birds, stands the older Freija kasbah, now uninhabited.

Edge of the vast Souss Massa National Park

lined with cafés and shops. Renowned crafters still work with silver here, producing lovely Amazigh jewellery and sabres with inlaid handles.

9. Sidi Ifni
This colonial-style town sits on the crest of a rocky plateau overlooking the Atlantic. To get here, follow the scenic road from Tiznit. Formerly a Spanish coastal enclave, Sidi Ifni has maintained an Iberian feel and is a popular surfing hub today.

10. Tafraoute
◙ B3
At an altitude of 1,200 m (3,938 ft), Tafraoute stands in the heart of a stunning valley in the Anti-Atlas. The palm groves here are lush and when they flower in February, the almond trees are covered with clouds of dusky pink and white blossom. The town is the territory of the Ameln, the best-known of the six tribes of the Anti-Atlas. They are renowned for their skill as traders. Tafraoute is also a centre for the manufacture of round-toe, leather slippers.

6. Souss Massa National Park
◙ A3
This park extends along the banks of Wadi Massa, which contains reed beds inhabited by large flocks of flamingoes from Camargue and Spain and the endangered northern bald ibis. The best time to see the birds is early in the morning, from March to April and October to November.

7. Agadir
◙ A3
Flattened by a terrible earthquake in 1960, Agadir was rebuilt and is now a thriving charter tourist resort. Its gentle climate, sheltered beach and many hotels draw thousands of visitors a year, making it Morocco's second most popular city after Marrakech.

8. Tiznit
◙ A3
In this small town, surrounded by pink *pisé* ramparts, visitors feel the proximity of both the Atlantic and the desert. Its central *méchouar* parade ground is

Rocky outcrop towering over Tafraoute

TIZI-N-TICHKA PASS

The N9 highway runs southeast from Marrakech over the Atlas Mountains, crossing the country's highest pass. On the other side, it then descends to the town of Ouarzazate, considered the gateway to the Sahara. Along the way, travellers will come across interesting sights, including the kasbahs of Telouet and Aït Benhaddou. The route is 196-km (122-miles) long and there are some stretches that demand careful driving; as a result, the journey can take nearly four hours. Travellers can hire a *grand taxi* or a car, or take a bus; several buses run from Marrakech's bus station. Transport company Supratours also runs daily trips to Ouarzazate.

1 Aït Ourir
C1

This rural town, at the foot of the Atlas Mountains, is located 35 km (22 miles) outside Marrakech. It becomes more active on Fridays, when farmers trade camels, sheep and other agricultural produce in a weekly country market. If visitors pass through on the right day, it makes for a great hour-long stop off.

2 Taddert
C1

After Aït Ourir, the last stop before the pass is the village of Taddert. In the higher part of the settlement, a handful of good cafés offer beautiful views of the valley below. When the pass is closed due to bad weather conditions, a barrier is lowered to halt all traffic.

1 Top 10 Sights
p100

(1) The Valley of the Kasbahs
p104

For places to see in this area, see p117

The spectacular Tizi-n-Tichka Pass

3 Tizi-n-Tichka Pass
🗺 C2

As the road leaves Taddert, the green landscape turns scenically rugged and barren, the twisting, precipitous drops keeping drivers focused. At its highest point, the pass peaks at 2,260 m (7,415 ft), making it the highest road pass in Morocco. Here, the road is marked by no more than a few stalls selling colourful rocks found in the region. While some of these rocks are fake, the real ones reveal glittering crystal formations when broken.

4 Kasbah Taourirt
🗺 D2 🕐 8am–5pm daily 🔗

The main landmark of Ouarzazate, this large kasbah used to belong to the Glaoui tribe. Parts are still inhabited, while other sections have been carefully restored. Its atmospheric, narrow alleys evoke a sense of what life here was like in the 19th century.

5 Kasbah Tifoultoute
🗺 D2 🕐 8am–5pm daily

Tifoultoute is another kasbah that once belonged to the Glaoui, and is situated just outside of Ouarzazate. Although parts of it are crumbling away, one section has been rebuilt and serves as a hotel and restaurant.

Lovely central courtyard at Kasbah Tifoultoute

A film set at the famous Atlas Corporation Studios

6 Atlas Corporation Studios

📍 D2 📞 0524 88 22 12 🕐 8:15am–6:45pm daily 🅿️ ♿

Ouarzazate has become the centre of the Moroccan film industry and is home to the Atlas Corporation Studios. Found 6 km (4 miles) to the north of town, the studios were built to provide infrastructure, sound stages and sets for movies; films shot here include *Gladiator* and *Kingdom of Heaven*, as well as episodes of the world-famous *Game of Thrones*. Film buffs can see sets here such as the Egyptian temple from the French production of *Asterix and Cleopatra*. The studios also offer guided tours, which run every 20 to 40 minutes. A shuttle bus runs between the studio and avenue Mohammed V.

7 Ouarzazate

📍 D2

The so-called "Gateway to the Sahara" (pronounced "war-zazat") is a town of around 60,000 people. Most visitors tend to spend at least one night here before pushing on south to the desert proper, or heading east to the Dadès Gorge (p104) and beyond. The number of hotels in town is always increasing and the quality is constantly improving. There are plenty of interesting activities in the area: from camel-trekking and quad biking to desert safaris and guided tours of the Atlas film studios for which the town is renowned.

8 Valley of the Kasbahs

From Ouarzazate, visitors can continue east through the Skoura Valley along a road dotted with oases and the ancient mud-brick strongholds that give the route its more romantic nickname (p104). The road eventually runs out at Merzouga, 350 miles (562 km) from Marrakech, and there is nothing to be found between here and the Algerian border but sand dunes.

9 Aït Benhaddou

📍 D2

This sprawling kasbah features on UNESCO's list of World Heritage Sites and is one of the best preserved in the region. It is also among the most famous, and, thanks to its popularity with visiting film producers and directors, it has been immortalized in dozens of Hollywood movies, including *Lawrence of Arabia*, *The Last Temptation of Christ*, *The Mummy*, *Gladiator* and *Alexander*. Part of its appeal lies in its location, with the kasbah tumbling down a hillside beside the Ouarzazate River. The kasbah is still partially inhabited by a few families.

Fortified cluster of kasbahs at Aït Benhaddou

THAMI EL GLAOUI

In 1893, the Glaoui tribe of Telouet was rewarded for rescuing Sultan Moulay Hassan and his army from a blizzard. They benefited further after the French took over – Thami El Glaoui was made *pasha* (lord) and became one of the most powerful men in the country. Hated for his support of the French, he died soon after Morocco gained independence in 1956.

10 Kasbah Telouet
🗺 C2

Dominated by a kasbah, the village of Telouet was once the stronghold of the Glaoui tribe, which, in the early 20th century, came to rule all of southern Morocco under French sponsorship. The Glaoui family dominated the salt trade due to the kasbah's location on the caravan trails near the major salt mines in the area. Abandoned for nearly half a century, much of the kasbah is now in a crumbling and dilapidated condition. However, you can visit the ornate reception hall and its rooftop terrace, which offers great views.

SOUTH TO THE DESERT

Day One

From **Ouarzazate**, the road continues south through the Draa Valley down to the administrative town of Zagora. After a drive of about four hours, stop at **Tamnougalt**, a dramatic *ksar* (fortified village) 10 minutes off the main road, 5 km (3 miles) after the small market town of Agdz. Further south is Kasbah Timiderte, a fortress from the Glaoui era. **Zagora** itself is dominated by **Jbel Zagora**.

The lively market, held on Wednesdays and Sundays, teems with dates that grow in abundance here. Just south of the centre is the hamlet of Amezrou. Nearby, the Kasbah des Juifs is inhabited by Amazigh silversmiths. Zagora's most famous attraction is a sign with a camel caravan that reads "Timbuktu, 52 Days".

Day Two

The village of M'Hamid is 96 km (60 miles) further south of Zagora. En route, **Tamegroute's** mosque-and-shrine complex is off limits to non-Muslims, except for the library with its collection of ancient manuscripts. Drive 5 km (3 miles) further on and you will see the first of the Tinfou Dunes. The best dunes can be accessed from **M'Hamid**, a sleepy outpost at the road's end – a one-street settlement that feels like it is at the end of the world.

The Valley of the Kasbahs

1. Skoura
▼ D2

Skoura, the first town east of Ouarzazate, has a delightfully slow pace of life. It is notable for a *palmeraie* with old kasbahs including the Kasbah Amridil (part hotel, part museum), once owned by the Glaoui family. The kasbah's restored interior is now open to visitors. On Mondays and Thursdays, the town's souks offer an array of exciting local produce.

2. Dadès Gorge
▼ E1

Follow the road north from Boumalne Dadès to this incredible gorge, which stands out against the rocky landscape. The cultivated land on the banks of the Wadi Dadès is surrounded by almond, fig and walnut trees, and poplars.

3. Kalaat M'Gouna
▼ D2

This small town, whose name means "fortress", lies at the heart of rose-growing country. In the 10th century, pilgrims returning from Mecca brought *rosa damascena* back with them to Morocco. These peppery scented flowers have developed a resistance to the cold and dry conditions in

which they are now grown. Most of the petals picked each spring are exported around the world for use in the perfume industry.

4. Merzouga
▼ F2

The small Saharan oasis of Merzouga is famous for its location at the foot of the Erg Chebbi dunes. At sunrise or dusk, the half-light gives the sand a fascinating range of colours. Merzouga attracts hundreds of pink flamingos, storks and other migratory birds. Camel drivers offer one-hour to two-day desert tours of the area.

5. Tinerhir
▼ E1

This lively town, built on a rocky outcrop, is bordered by lush palm groves. With several working silver mines in the vicinity, Tinerhir is known for its jewellery. To the southeast is Aït el-Haj Ali, the former *mellah* (Jewish quarter), whose houses make an interesting architectural ensemble.

6. Goulmima
▼ E1

In the heart of the Rheris oasis, several fortified villages, or *ksours*, surround

The beautiful Kasbah Amridil in the oasis of Skoura

the village of Goulmima. Their towers are remarkably high and, when tribal feuds were rife, they protected the inhabitants against the incursions of the Aït Atta, who came to pillage their harvests. A walled town east of the Erfoud road is worth a detour.

7. Errachidia
🅟 F1
As a result of its strategic location between northern and southern Morocco, and between the Atlantic seaboard, Figuig and the Algerian border, Errachidia became the main town in the province. The palm groves of the Ziz and Tafilalt begin from here. This town is also known for its pottery.

8. Erfoud
🅟 F1
This town serves as a base for tours to the Erg Chebbi sand dunes and the Tafilalt palm grove. It also hosts a three-day Date Festival each October following the date harvest.

9. Rissani
🅟 F1
This ancient town dating back to the 7th century lies on the edge of the Sahara and has a very famous souk. To the east is the Hammada du Guir, a stony desert known for its sandstorms.

10. Todra Gorge
🅟 E1
Sheer cliffs rise up from this narrow gorge with Tamtattouchte village at the northern end. These are the most impressive cliffs in southern Morocco, and they are well known to experienced mountaineers. There are a couple of good hotels here for overnight stays.

Wadi Todra flowing through the Todra Gorge

STREETSMART

Serving Moroccan mint tea

GETTING AROUND

Whether exploring Marrakech by foot or making use of public transport, here is everything you need to know to navigate the city and the areas beyond the centre like a pro.

AT A GLANCE

TRAVEL COSTS

MARRAKECH CITY CENTRE

10 Dh

Single *petit taxi* journey within the city

MARRAKECH TO ESSAOUIRA

95 Dh

Single bus journey

MARRAKECH TO OUARZAZATE

100 Dh

Place in a *grand taxi*

SPEED LIMITS

AUTOROUTES

120 km/h (75 mph)

NATIONAL ROADS

100 km/h (60 mph)

URBAN AREAS

60 km/h (35 mph)

Arriving by Air

Marrakech is served by **Marrakech Airport** (RAK), which is just 5 km (3 miles) from the Medina. Taxis can be found outside the arrivals hall, although prices for these are massively inflated – either head to the taxi booking counter in the airport to prepay your fare or try the taxis in the car park instead. It is advisable that you agree a price with your driver before setting off.

There is also a bus (No 19) that departs every 30 minutes and runs to Jemaa el-Fna via all the large hotels.
Marrakech Airport
w marrakeshairport.info

Train Travel

The train network in Morocco is not extensive but the service is excellent. Train services from Casablanca, Fès, Rabat and Tangier arrive at Marrakech's **ONCF Railway Station**. From the station it is a short walk into central Guéliz, or a ten-minute taxi ride to Jemaa el-Fna for the Medina.
ONCF Railway Station
w oncf.ma

Bus Travel

Long-distance buses connect all major towns and cities. The main operators are **CTM** and **Supratours**. The buses are comfortable and cheap. On busy routes, such as Marrakech–Essaouira and Casablanca–Marrakech, book a few days ahead.
CTM
w ctm.ma
Supratours
w supratours.ma

Grand Taxi

An alternative to the long-distance bus is the *grand taxi*, or shared taxi. These are traditionally Mercedes saloons, although they are increasingly being replaced by people carriers, and operate like minibuses. They gather near bus stations or public squares with their destinations posted in the window or shouted out by the driver. Once the vehicle has filled up with passengers it leaves. *Grands taxis* often ply routes that are not well-served by buses, including over the Tizi-n-Test and Tizi-n-Tichka passes. Be aware that usage of seatbelts is rare and drivers often don't adhere to speed limits.

Petit Taxi

Regular taxis (as opposed to *grands taxis*) are known as *petits taxis and* are used for short-distance journeys. They are usually small cars taking only three passengers and can be flagged down on the street. These taxis often do not have meters and it is necessary to negotiate a fixed price in advance with the driver. To avoid paying more than you need to, ask at your hotel what the correct fares are for local journeys. *Petits taxis* are not permitted to carry passengers beyond the limits of the city in which they operate. If you want to make a daytrip out of town you need to hire a *grand taxi*.

Calèches

Horse-drawn open carriages, or *calèches*, are used almost exclusively by tourists taking sightseeing trips. Before embarking on a ride, check that the driver is licensed with SPANA, an international charity that oversees the welfare of working animals.
SPANA
w spana.org

Cycling

Marrakech's roads can be chaotic and so cycling is perhaps best undertaken by experienced cyclists. Others may be interested in taking a guided bike tour, such as those offered by **Pikala Bikes**.

Pikala Bikes
w pikalabikes.com

Walking

Marrakech is small and the best way to get around is on foot. In fact, in the Medina you have no choice, as Jemaa el-Fna and many other areas are off limits to cars. This does not, however, prevent scooters and bicycles careering through the alleys, ignoring the signs forbidding such vehicles. The network of streets is labyrinthine and street signs are few so expect to get lost a lot. When you do, don't panic: you will never be more than a few minutes' walk from somewhere familiar.

The walk to Guéliz, beyond the old city walls, takes about 20 minutes.

Travelling Outside the City

For excursions outside of Marrakech, to neighbouring cities, the countryside or to the Atlas Mountains, take a CTM or Supratours bus, *grand taxi* or car.

A car is the easiest way to explore beyond the city. One option is to hire a car and driver. This gives you complete flexibility. Most hotels can organize this for you. You can also hire a car and drive yourself – most major international car hire companies are represented in Marrakech. Car hire is quite expensive, with local agencies charging around 400 Dh a day. Check the terms of your agreement carefully, especially clauses relating to insurance and cover in case of accident or theft. A 4WD car is a must for heading south over the Atlas Mountains as roads are often steep and the terrain is rocky.

The Moroccan highway code is similar to that of France, so drive on the right and give way to traffic on the right at roundabouts and junctions. Road signs are in Arabic and French.

GETTING TO AND FROM THE AIRPORT			
Airport	**Transport**	**Journey Time**	**Price**
Marrakech Airport	Taxi	15 mins	70 Dh
	Bus No 19	40 mins	30 Dh

PRACTICAL INFORMATION

A little local know-how goes a long way in Marrakech. On these pages you can find all the essential advice and information you will need to make the most of your trip to this city.

AT A GLANCE

CURRENCY
Dirham

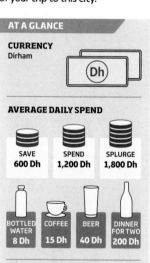

AVERAGE DAILY SPEND

SAVE	SPEND	SPLURGE
600 Dh	1,200 Dh	1,800 Dh

BOTTLED WATER	COFFEE	BEER	DINNER FOR TWO
8 Dh	15 Dh	40 Dh	200 Dh

ESSENTIAL PHRASES

Hello	As-salaam aleikum
Goodbye	B'salaama
Please	Afak
Thank you	Shukran
Do you speak English?	Itkelim Ingleezi?
I don't understand...	Mafayimtish

ELECTRICITY SUPPLY

Power sockets are type C and E, fitting two-pronged plugs. The standard voltage is 220 volts.

Passports and Visas

For entry requirements, including visas, consult your nearest Moroccan embassy or check the Moroccan **Ministry of Foreign Affairs** website. Citizens of the UK, EU, Switzerland, the US, Canada, Australia and New Zealand need a valid passport to visit Morocco, but a visa is not required. To be able to stay for up to 90 days, your passport should be valid for at least three months post your date of arrival. If your stay exceeds 90 days, then you must get an extension from the central police station.
Ministry of Foreign Affairs
Ⓦ consulat.ma

Government Advice

It is important to consult both your and the Moroccan government's advice before travelling. The UK Foreign, Commonwealth and Development Office (**FCDO**), the **US Department of State**, the **Australian Department of Foreign Affairs and Trade** and **Visit Morocco** (the national tourist board) offer the latest information on security, health and local regulations.
Australian Department of Foreign Affairs and Trade
Ⓦ smartraveller.gov.au
FCDO
Ⓦ gov.uk/foreign-traveladvice
US Department of State
Ⓦ travel.state.gov
Visit Morocco
Ⓦ visitmorocco.com

Customs Information

You can find information on the laws relating to goods and currency taken in or out of Morocco on the **Customs and Excise Administration** website.
Customs and Excise Administration
Ⓦ douane.gov.ma

Insurance

We recommend that you take out a comprehensive insurance policy covering theft, loss of belongings, medical care, cancellations and delays, and read the small print carefully. Morocco does not have any reciprocal health care agreements with other countries, so taking out full medical insurance is important.

Vaccinations

There are no required vaccinations for Morocco, although inoculations against hepatitis A and B and typhoid, which can all be contracted in Morocco through contaminated food or water, are advised.

Money

Debit cards and credit cards such as Visa and MasterCard are accepted in most shops and restaurants. American Express is less widely accepted. Credit cards often attract a surcharge of 5 per cent. ATMs are widely available in Marrakech and neighbouring towns and cities. It is always worth carrying some cash, as many small businesses and markets still only accept cash.

Tipping is an ingrained part of Moroccan society. Almost any service rendered will warrant a tip, known as *baksheesh*. Keep a stash of small denomination notes for this purpose. A tip of 10–15 per cent of the total bill is expected in restaurants; hotel porters will expect 1 dh per bag and housekeeping a tip of 5–10 Dh per day; round up *petit taxis* fares to the nearest dirham and tip 10 per cent of a *grand taxi* fare.

Travellers with Specific Requirements

Those with limited mobility will find Marrakech tricky to navigate, especially in the Medina where the crowded roads tend to be narrow and in poor condition. There is little adapted infrastructure such as wheelchair-friendly ramps, signs in Braille, or beeping and flashing pedestrian crossings. Beyond the large hotels and the railway station, very few buildings are accessible, though the city's better riads will do their best to assist. On the plus side, Moroccans are extremely accommodating and resourceful, and do their best to make things as easy as possible. The **Disabled Tourist Guide** website offers information and advice on travel in Morocco for those with specific requirements.
Disabled Tourist Guide
🅦 disabled-touristguide.com

Language

French and Arabic are the main languages. Tamazight, the language of the Amazigh people, is also used in the city. English is spoken widely by those working in the tourism industry.

Opening Hours

Although a Muslim country, much of Morocco follows a Monday to Friday working week. Business hours for banks are 8:15am–3:45pm Monday to Friday (9:30am–2pm during Ramadan). Shops open up a bit later but stay open until 8pm or 9pm. Some shops in the souks shut at lunch on Fridays.

On Saturdays many businesses open for half a day and on Sundays all public businesses and banks are closed, as are many shops.

Most places close early or for the day on public holidays.

During the religious festivals of Eid El Fitr and Eid El Adha, the city stays shut for a minimum of two days, so travelling is very difficult. In the holy month of Ramadan (begins 1 March in 2025 and 18 February in 2026, and lasts for 30 days) many Muslims fast during the day; due to this, many restaurants and eateries are closed until sundown. Some restaurants may also abstain from serving alcohol at this time.

Situations can change quickly and unexpectedly. Always check before visiting attractions and hospitality venues for up-to-date opening hours and booking requirements.

Personal Security

Marrakech is generally a safe place, but petty crime does take place. Beware of pickpockets in crowded tourist areas, particularly in the souks and on Jemaa el-Fna. Bag-snatching thieves operate on scooters, so be vigilant. Use your common sense, keep your belongings close and be alert to your surroundings. If you have anything stolen, report the crime as soon as possible at the nearest office of the tourist police (Brigade Touristique). Get a copy of the crime report to claim on your insurance. Contact your embassy or consulate if your passport is stolen or in the event of a serious crime or accident.

Homosexuality is illegal in Morocco, and is technically punishable by up to three years of imprisonment. However, this is rarely enforced, and this law does not apply to non-Moroccan same-sex partners visiting the country. It is strongly advised that all travellers use discretion, regardless of sexual orientation. Public displays of affection by anyone are generally frowned upon, and should be avoided.

Health

Morocco has both a public and a private healthcare system. Generally speaking, treatment in private hospitals is of a higher standard than that given in the under-funded public sector. In an emergency, don't wait for an ambulance. Flag a taxi and go to the nearest private hospital. You will have to pay for medical treatment on the spot, including any supplies used. Keep receipts to claim the cost from your insurance company later.

For minor ailments go to a pharmacy or chemist, which are usually very well stocked and have knowledgeable staff. If you have an accident or medical problem requiring non-urgent medical attention, ask at your hotel for a doctor.

Smoking, Alcohol and Drugs

Moroccan law prohibits smoking in most public buildings but this is rarely enforced.

Although Muslims are forbidden to drink alcohol, Morocco is a moderate Islamic country. It has a few bars and most restaurants, especially those frequented by foreigners, serve beer, wine and spirits.

While hashish, known locally as *kif*, is illegal, plenty of Moroccans smoke it.

AT A GLANCE

EMERGENCY NUMBERS

POLICE

19

AMBULANCE & FIRE SERVICE

150

TIME ZONE
CET
(GMT +1)
There is no daylight saving time.

TAP WATER
It is best to avoid drinking tap water. Many esablishments serve filtered water to limit the use of plastic bottles.

WEBSITES AND APPS

Visit Marrakech
Official visitor website and app for Marrakech (*visitmarrakech.com*) providing plenty of useful tourist information.

CTM app
This app is the best way to purchase tickets for CTM buses.

Visit Morocco
Morocco's official tourist board website (*visitmorocco.com*) gives excellent recommendations for accomodation, tours and trips.

visitors may well be offered *kif* for sale, but the penalty for buying or smoking it is ten years' imprisonment.

ID

Visitors to Morocco are not required to carry ID, but it is a good idea to keep a photocopy of the information pages of your passport on your person.

Responsible Travel

The climate crisis is having a big impact on Marrakech, with increasingly frequent droughts and heatwaves. Do your bit by taking quick showers and reusing towels if staying in a hotel. Refill bottles if your accommodation has filtered water.

Shopping Tips

Bargaining is a standard process when shopping, but more and more places are moving to fixed prices. When bargaining, offering half or two-thirds of the asking price is a good place to start. If you manage to get a good deal, you may feel that you have undercut the seller – don't worry, they wouldn't sell it if they weren't making a profit.

You may be approached in the Medina by people offering their services as guides. Always check that they are licensed before hiring them. Any discount that a guide may obtain for you at shops will be negated by their own commission, which the shopkeeper will factor into the price of goods, so be sure to bargain when making purchases. Alternatively, your hotel can organize an official guide for you or book with a reputable company such as **Marrakech Guided Tours** or **Travel Link**.
Marrakech Guided Tours
Ⓦ marrakechguidedtours.com
Travel Link
Ⓦ travellink.ma

Local Customs

Islam is the state religion and the king of Morocco is the leader of the faithful. It is therefore considered in bad taste to criticize religion. It is also ill-mannered to disturb someone while they are at prayer. The fast of Ramadan is strictly observed in Morocco, and many dining establishments close during daylight hours as a result; non-Muslims should avoid eating, drinking and smoking in public during the day.

Because Morocco is conservative, with a mostly Muslim population, visitors should dress modestly. In practice, this means covering the shoulders and not wearing shorts. Dresses and skirts should be at least knee length. It is not necessary to cover your hair.

The Indigenous people of North Africa, known as Berbers throughout most of history, prefer to call themselves Amazigh, meaning "free people". The name "Berber" was given to the Amazigh people by the Romans, was perpetuated by Arab invaders and used by the French in the early 20th century. The Amazigh people in Morocco continue to agitate for the acknowledgment of their identity and culture, and some progress has been made, including the recognition of their language, Tamazight, as an official language of Morocco in 2011.

Mobile Phones and Wi-Fi

Operators Maroc-Télécom, Meditél and INWI have arrangements with European networks that allow visitors to use their home mobile networks in Morocco. If visiting for a long period, it is best to buy a pre-paid SIM card from a local provider.

Many hotels and riads offer free Wi-Fi, as do many restaurants and cafés, and there are free Wi-Fi hotspots at most train and bus stations.

Postal Services

Main post offices are operated by Poste Maroc. Buy stamps at *tabacs*, small tobacco and newspaper kiosks.

Taxes and Refunds

VAT of 20 per cent is levied on most goods and services. Visitors may be eligible for a refund on presentation of a receipt for purchases of over 2,000 Dh. This service is available at Marrakech airport.

PLACES TO STAY

From authentic riads lit by candle to opulent palaces fit for royalty, the accommodation in Marrakech is as vibrant as the Medina. You can relax in a riad – a house centred around a courtyard – amid the hustle and bustle of Jemaa el Fna or stay off the beaten track in an ecolodge high in the Atlas Mountains.

September to May is the best but busiest time to visit, and peak holiday dates will incur higher prices. Summer is very hot and winter can get cold at night, so check for air con and heating accordingly.

PRICE CATEGORIES

For a standard, double room per night (with breakfast if included), taxes and extra charges.

Dh under 1,200 Dh
Dh Dh 1,200–2,500 Dh
Dh Dh Dh over 2,500 Dh

Jemaa el-Fna and the Kasbah

Villa des Orangers

📍 J5 🏠 6 Rue Sidi Mimoun
🌐 villadesorangers.com
· Dh Dh Dh

Welcome to a five-star hotel that feels like a private home. This luxurious oasis offers serenity and privacy across three adjoining riads where courtyards are flush with citrus trees. Three pools, one heated for cooler winter days, and two delightful restaurants round out the hospitable comforts. Located between Jemaa el-Fna and the Kasbah district, the villa is a stone's throw from both.

La Sultana

📍 K6 🏠 403 Rue de la Kasbah 🌐 lasultana hotels.com · Dh Dh Dh

It's all about the little details at this luxury boutique hotel, from the hand-carved, ornate architecture to the impeccable service delivered by staff. A stunning roof terrace heightens the experience,

as does the exquisite in-house spa featuring traditional *hammams* and spaces to relax.

Les Jardins de la Koutoubia

📍 J3 🏠 26 Rue de La Koutoubia 🌐 lesjardins delahoutoubia.com · Dh Dh

This popular, centrally located hotel overlooks the Koutoubia Mosque and sits adjacent to the Jemaa el-Fna. More than 100 rooms are available, including suites that highlight its prime location with views of the Medina or Koutoubia Minaret. After a day of exploring, you won't be far from the hotel pools, spa or peaceful rooftop.

Riad Noos Noos

📍 L5 🏠 8 Derb Jemaa Lahbir 🌐 riadnoosnoos. com · Dh

Partake in the traditional home-away-from-home riad experience in this charming guesthouse. Families are well-catered to: two of the nine individually appointed rooms are family suites and the riad features a

billiards room, board games and a library sure to delight children and parents alike.

The Souks

Central House Marrakech

📍 K1 🏠 Medina Amssafah 32 🌐 thecentralhousehost els.com/marrakech · Dh

For solo travellers looking for a friendly and stylish hostel, Central House delivers on all fronts with its sunny roof terrace, courtyard pool and bustling café full of like-minded adventurers. Its mix of private and shared rooms are clean and comfortable, with privacy curtains and plenty of plug sockets.

La Maison Arabe

📍 H2 🏠 1 Derb Assehbé, Bab Douhhala 🌐 cenizaro. com/lamaisonarabe · Dh Dh

This historic luxury hotel claims to be Morocco's first boutique riad and is ideal for foodie travellers. Here, you can take a class at the hotel's cookery school, which dates back to 1946, choosing from half-day workshops or five-day courses. Some are held at its swanky country club, 15 minutes outside the city, via the hotel's free shuttle.

Dar Attajmil

📍 J3 🏠 23 Souh Lahsour, 🌐 darattajmil.com · Ⓓ①Ⓓ①

This elegant riad promises great value for money and an intimate stay. Home to only four guest rooms, expect a cosy, personalized experience. The pretty rooftop and private *hammam* are designed for relaxation while fantastic in-house dining and cookery classes are lovely social options.

Riad Kniza

📍 H2 🏠 14 Derb l'Hotel, Bab Doukhala 🌐 riad hniza.com · Ⓓ①Ⓓ①

Dating back to the 18th century, this authentic riad has been in the same family for nearly 200 years. The owners' private collection of art and cultural pieces has been curated into a fascinating on-site museum for guests to peruse. Attentive English-speaking staff are on hand to fulfil your palatial holiday home experience.

El Fenn

📍 J3 🏠 Derb Moulay Abdullah Ben Hezzian, 2 🌐 el-fenn.com · Ⓓ①Ⓓ①Ⓓ①

A perfect one for design enthusiasts: this flamboyant boutique

has a collection of individually styled rooms. Bold colours and contemporary artworks are matched by luxurious fabrics and relaxed vibes. The sprawling rooftop terrace is a popular spot for sunset cocktails thanks to its close-up view of the Koutoubia Mosque and its friendly team of mixologists.

Le Farnatchi

📍 K2 🏠 Derb el Farnatchi, Rue Souh el Fassis 🌐 le farnatchi.com · Ⓓ①Ⓓ①Ⓓ①

As one of the original riad hotels in the city, Le Farnatchi is a study in elegant tradition. The innovatively curated suites have fresh white walls, antique furniture and intricate, hand-carved details. The communal areas are spacious and beautiful, and with direct access to the adjacent Farnatchi Spa you're mere moments away from some serious RnR.

Riad Alena

📍 J3 🏠 35 Derb Jdid 🌐 riadalenamarrakech. com · Ⓓ①Ⓓ①

This well-priced riad is run by a friendly family of hoteliers and art lovers, whose influence is seen in the traditional decor and lively pops of colour throughout the comfortable rooms. Their attention to detail extends to the delicious, free breakfast served on the rooftop terrace, homemade by the family.

Riad Adore

📍 J2 🏠 97 Derb Tizouagrine, Dar El Bacha 🌐 riadadore.com · Ⓓ①Ⓓ①

Whitewashed walls and soft grey hand-carved wooden shutters create a peaceful backdrop for this tranquil oasis. Elegant, modern room interiors and mindfully curated lounges and terraces elevate the calm atmosphere. With great service, delicious breakfasts and on-site spas, it's excellent value for your money.

Riad Linda

📍 K3 🏠 93 Derb Jamaa, Derb Dabachi 🌐 iadlinda. com · Ⓓ①

Enjoy a warm welcome at this affordable option in a central location, just five minutes from Jemaa el-Fna square. The multi-lingual staff will have a cup of mint tea ready for you upon arrival and will be on hand to cater to all your needs throughout your stay, from transport to dining.

Royal Mansour

📍 G4 🏠 Rue Abou Abbas El Sebti 🌐 royalmansour. com · Ⓓ①Ⓓ①

For palatial opulence book here: the hotel is owned by the royal family. Each enchanting, stand-alone riad is spread over three floors and has a private butler. The exquisite spa is one of the world's leading wellness centres, with signature *hammam* treatments fit for a king.

Riad Dyor

☑ F3 ☖ 1 Driba Jdida
🌐 ryaddyor.com · ⓑⓑ

Luxuriate in this romantic hideaway that includes decadent decor and original features; the hand-painted ceilings date back 300 years. The sumptuous suites feature freestanding bathtubs or private fireplaces. Exceptional hospitality and genuine warmth create a welcome retreat for guests amid the hustle and bustle of the Medina. A *hammam*, splash pool and rooftop dining complete the idyllic experience.

La Mamounia

☑ F3 ☖ Avenue Bad Jdid
🌐 mamounia.com · ⓑⓑⓑ

What do Winston Churchill, Paul McCartney and the Rolling Stones all have in common? They all stayed at this iconic 1920s palace hotel. Aside from its celebrity visitor book, this hotel captures the hearts of those who have stayed here with its timeless elegance. Steeped in history and luxury, enjoy the comfy rooms, fine dining, deluxe spa and Hollywood-level service.

The New City

Es Saadi Hotel Hivernage

☑ C6 ☖ Rue Ibrahim El Mazini, Hivernage
🌐 essaadi.com · ⓑⓑ

For a reasonably priced family-friendly option, look no further than this resort. Families can be comfortable in triple rooms or bungalows, and children will love the lush gardens, swimming pools and Kids' Club. As a bonus, it's a family-run business with real eco-credentials: they utilize water recycling for the gardens and the organic farm provides fruit, vegetables and poultry to the hotel's multiple restaurants.

Sofitel Marrakech

☑ C6 ☖ Rue Haroun Errachid 🌐 sofitel-marrakech.com · ⓑⓑⓑ

You may be familiar with this chain hotel and its extensive facilities: quality dining, a fitness centre, outdoor pools and multilingual staff. Its leafy gardens provide tranquillity in the day, while at night, the terrace bar comes to life with a local and international party crowd. What more could you want?

Maison Brummell Majorelle

☑ C4 ☖ 7 Rue Al Madina 🌐 maisonbrummell-majorelle.brummell-projects.com · ⓑⓑ

Architecture and design lovers are sure to like this urban oasis adjacent to the Jardins Majorelle. The minimalist bedrooms have polished cream walls, terrazzo floors and thick wool rugs, and the friendly, switched-on staff invite you to feel at home. Breakfasts are a communal affair on the dreamy patio.

Nobu

☑ C6 ☖ Av. Echouhada et Rue du Temple 🌐 marrahech.nobuhotels.com · ⓑⓑ

Calling all glamorous globetrotters: reserve a spot at the first Nobu in Africa. The all-suite five-star hotel has a rooftop with a pool, bar and beach club vibes in addition to epic city and Atlas Mountain views. It's a perfect stay for those who appreciate quality service and exceptional food, including Nobu's signature New-Style Japanese cuisine.

Dar Rhizlane

☑ C6 ☖ Avenue Jnane el Harti 🌐 dar-rhizlane.com · ⓑⓑⓑ

This elegant and romantic villa within lush gardens is a perfect choice for couples with refined taste. Each room, named for a Moroccan perfume, is spacious and uniquely decorated, opening out onto flower-filled terraces or fragrant gardens. The hotel's facilities include a professional kitchen for private cookery classes, a luxurious spa and a fine dining restaurant.

Tizi-n-Test Pass

Kasbah du Toubkal

☑ C2 ☖ Toubhal National Park, Imlil 🌐 hasbah toubhal.com · ⓑⓑ

For hiking enthusiasts and nature lovers, book into this ecolodge perched upon a hilltop. A mountain refuge with epic views, this lodge has cosy ensuite bedrooms and is a short walk – or mule ride – from Imlil village. It has been awarded a Green Globe for its efforts towards sustainable tourism and is staffed by locals from the surrounding villages.

Kasbah Tamadot

C2 **Asni** **virgin limitededition.com/ kasbah-tamadot**

Disconnect from daily life and tune into nature at Sir Richard Branson's award-winning luxury mountain retreat. If you are able to drag yourself away from the pool and its jaw-dropping views of the Atlas Mountains, you can embark on a hike right from the doorstep. Choose from suites in the kasbah, exquisitely outfitted glamper tents or one of the three-bedroom riads, ideal for large groups and families.

Douar Samra

C2 **Tamatert, Toubkal National Park** **douar-samra.net**

Experience hearty Amazigh hospitality and rural life in the Toubkal National Park. Built with natural materials, there's an earthy feel throughout the property. Rooms in the main house don't have electricity but are lit with candles and oil lamps, though family rooms and Scandi-style treehouse options do have electricity. Go for a nearby hike, or enjoy the view from the gardens and terraces.

Palais Oumensour

B2 **Borj Oumensour, Taroudant** **palais oumensour.com**

This beautiful palace retreat is in the heart of Taroudant city, nick-named the "grandmother of Marrakech". Its lush, peaceful gardens with a decently sized, refreshing pool are a relaxing place to unwind after a busy morning in the city's souks. The rooms are excellent value for money too, as is the delicious set dinner menu.

Auberge Le Mouflon

C2 **Ouirgane**

Located within a rural Atlas Mountains community, this family-run guesthouse brings with it a warm, authentic Amazigh welcome. Hearty home-cooked tagines eaten as part of the family in the morning will set you up for a whole day of activities at high altitude, while pretty gardens, ideal for relaxing, await when you return.

Ouirgane Ecolodge

C2 **Maghira, Ouirgane** **ouirgane-ecolodge.com**

For families seeking adventure in the Atlas Mountains, look no further. This ecolodge is designed with a focus on sustainability; it uses solar power, recycled water and aims to support the local community. The air-

conditioned rooms include family-sized spaces perfect for resting after a day of adventure. The hotel offers multi-day treks, mountain biking and yoga retreats.

Tizi-n-Tichka Pass

Kasbah Ait Ben Damiette

D2 **kasbahaitben-damiette.resa-manage ment.ma**

Nestled under a canopy of palms at the foot of the Atlas Mountains, this sensitively converted kasbah is an oasis for travellers. Refuel with a home-cooked meal prepared from a French-Moroccan menu or relax at the pool and gardens on your way to or from the Sahara desert.

Dar Ahlam Skoura

D2 **Douar Oulad Cheih Ali, Koucheït, Shoura** **darahlam.com**

This countryside kasbah's name translates from Arabic as "House of Dreams", and more than lives up to its name. The impeccable service and beautiful spaces make for a perfect mountain escape. This is a true luxury retreat for those who appreciate peace and privacy, and want to connect with nature while being spoiled by an outstanding staff. Indulge in experiences such as private dinners, outdoor massages and a night in a luxury tent beneath the open sky.

INDEX

FRENCH PHRASE BOOK

In Emergency

Help!	Au secours!	oh sekoor
Stop!	Arrêtez!	aret-ay
Call a doctor!	Appelez un médecin!	apuh-lay uñ medsañ
Call an ambulance!	Appelez une ambulance!	apuh-lay oon oñboo-loñs
Call the police!	Appelez la police!	apuh-lay lah poh-lees
Call the fire department!	Appelez les pompiers!	apuh-lay leh poñ-peeyay

Communication Essentials

Yes/No	Oui/Non	wee/noñ
Please	S'il vous plaît	seel voo play
Thank you	Merci	mer-see
Excuse me	Excusez-moi	exkoo-zay mwah
Hello	Bonjour	boñzhoor
Goodbye	Au revoir	oh ruh-vwar
Good evening	Bonsoir	boñ-swar
What?	Quoi?	kwah
When?	Quand?	koñ
Why?	Pourquoi?	poor-kwah
Where?	Où?	oo

Useful Phrases

How are you?	Comment allez-vous?	kom-moñ talay voo
Very well	Très bien	treh byañ
Pleased to meet you.	Enchanté	oñshoñ-tay
Where is/are…?	Où est/sont…?	oo ay/soñ
Which way to…?	Quelle est la direction pour…?	kel ay lah deer-ek-syoñ poor
Do you speak English?	Parlez-vous anglais?	par-lay voo oñg-lay
I don't understand.	Je ne comprends pas.	zhuh nuh kom-proñ pah
I'm sorry.	Excusez-moi.	exkoo-zay mwah

Useful Words

big	grand	groñ
small	petit	puh-tee
hot	chaud	show
cold	froid	frwah
good	bon	boñ
bad	mauvais	moh-veh
open	ouvert	oo-ver
closed	fermé	fer-meh
left	gauche	gohsh
right	droite	drwaht
entrance	l'entrée	l'on-tray
exit	la sortie	sor-tee
toilet	les toilettes	twah-let
Monday	lundi	luñ-dee
Tuesday	mardi	mar-dee
Wednesday	mercredi	mehrkruh-dee
Thursday	jeudi	zhuh-dee
Friday	vendredi	voñdruh-dee
Saturday	samedi	sam-dee
Sunday	dimanche	dee-moñsh

Shopping

How much does this cost?	C'est combien s'il vous plaît?	say kom-byañ seel voo play
I would like …	Je voudrais…	zhuh voo-dray
Do you have?	Est-ce que vous avez?	es-kuh voo zavay

Do you take credit cards?	Est-ce que vous acceptez les cartes de crédit?	es-kuh voo zaksept-ay leh kart duh kreh-dee
This one.	Celui-ci.	suhl-wee-see
That one.	Celui-là.	suhl-wee-lah
expensive	cher	shehr
cheap	pas cher, bon marché	pah shehr, boñ mar-shay

Sightseeing

art gallery	la galerie d'art	galer-ree dart
bus station	la gare routière	gahr roo-tee-yehr
garden	le jardin	zhar-dañ
mosque	la mosquée	mos-qay
museum	le musée	moo-zay
tourist information office	renseignements touristiques, le syndicat d'initiative	roñsayn-moñ toorees-teek, sandee-ka d'eenee-syateev
train station	la gare	gahr

Staying in a Hotel

Do you have a vacant room?	Est-ce que vous avez une chambre?	es-kuh voo-zavay oon shambr
double room, with double bed	chambre à deux personnes, avec un grand lit	shambr ah duh pehr-son, avek un gronñ lee
twin room	chambre à deux lits	shambr ah duh lee
single room	chambre à une personne	shambr ah oon pehr-son
room with a bath, shower	chambre avec salle de bains, une douche	shambr avek sal duh bañ, oon doosh
I have a reservation.	J'ai fait une réservation.	zhay fay oon rayzehrva-syoñ

Eating Out

Have you got a table?	Avez-vous une table libre?	avay-voo oon tahbl duh leebr
I want to reserve a table.	Je voudrais réserver une table.	zhuh voo-dray rayzehr-vay oon tahbl
The bill please.	L'addition s'il vous plaît.	l'adee-syoñ seel voo play
I am a vegetarian.	Je suis végétarien.	zhuh swee vezhay-tehryañ
menu	le menu, la carte	men-oo, karto
breakfast	le petit déjeuner	puh-tee deh-zhuh-nay
lunch	le déjeuner	deh-zhuh-nay
dinner	le dîner	dee-nay

Numbers

0	zéro	zeh-roh
1	un, une	uñ, oon
2	deux	duh
3	trois	trwah
4	quatre	katr
5	cinq	sañk
6	six	sees
7	sept	set
8	huit	weet
9	neuf	nerf
10	dix	dees

ARABIC PHRASE BOOK

Moroccan Arabic is unique to Morocco and is not understood by other Arabic speakers. Moroccans speak faster and abbreviate words. Pronunciation is gentler due to the influence of French.

In Emergency

Help!	*Aawenooni*
Stop!	*Owkof!*
Can you call a doctor?	*Momkin kellem el tabeeb?*
Call an ambulance!	*Aayeto aala el isaaf*
Can you call the police?	*Momkin kellem el polees?*
Call the fire department	*Aayeto aala el matafie*

Communication Essentials

Yes / No	*Na-am / Laa*
Please	*Min fadlak*
Thank you	*Se'hha*
Excuse me	*Min fadlak*
Hello / Peace be upon you	*Selaam*
Goodbye	*Ma'eel salaama*
Good morning	*Esbe'h elkheer*
Good evening	*Masaal kheer*
Today	*el yoom*
Yesterday	*el baareh*
Tomorrow	*Ghadan*
Tonight	*Felleel*
What?	*Shnoo?*
When?	*Imta?*
Why?	*Alash?*
Where?	*Fayn?*

Useful Phrases

How are you?	*Washraak?*
I'm fine.	*Laabas.*
Pleased to meet you.	*Metshar-fin*
Where is/are…?	*Fayn…?*
Which way to…?	*Ina terik…?*
Do you speak English?	*Tatkalam engleeze-ya?*
I don't understand	*Ana mafhimtaksh*
I'm sorry.	*Esme'hlee*

Useful Words

big	*kbeer*
small	*sgeer*
hot	*sokhoon*
cold	*baared*
good	*mlee'ha*
bad	*mashemlee'ha*
open	*maftoo'h*
closed	*maghlook*
left	*liseer*
right	*limeen*
entrance	*dokhool*
exit	*khrooj*
toilet	*towalett*
day	*nehaar*
week	*semaana*
Monday	*el etneen*
Tuesday	*el tlaata*
Wednesday	*el arbe'aa*
Thursday	*el khamees*
Friday	*el jomo'aa*
Saturday	*el sabet*
Sunday	*el a'had*

Shopping

How much is it?	*Kam else'er?*
I would like…	*Ana 'habbayt*
Do you have?	*Andak…?*
This one	*Hadi*
expensive	*ghaalya*
cheap	*rekheesa*

Sightseeing

art gallery	*galiree daar*
beach	*bhar*
bus station	*stasyon do boos*
garden	*eljonayna*
guide	*geed*
map	*kaart*
mosque	*masjid*
museum	*moozi*
park	*baark*
ticket	*tekee*
tourist office	*mektab soyaa'h*

Staying In a Hotel

Do you have a room?	*Enta 'andak ghorfa?*
double room	*ghorfa le shakhsayn*
single room	*ghorfa le shakhs waa'hid*
with bathroom / shower	*ma'al 'ham-maam/ doosh*
I have a reservation.	*Ana mereserve hna.*

Eating Out/Food

Have you got a table for…?	*Enta 'andak towla*
I want to reserve a table.	*Brit reservewahd tabla*
Can I have the bill please?	*Te'eteeni elfatoora min fadlak?*
I am a vegetarian.	*Ana nabati wa la akulu lehoum wala hout.*
breakfast	*iftar*
lunch	*reda*
dinner	*aasha*
steamed pot of vegetables with meat, etc	*tajeen*
hand-made couscous	*kuskus*
pastry filled with vegetables and meat, etc	*elbasteela*
soup	*'hreera*
meatballs with herbs	*kefta*
fish	*el'hoot*
chicken	*djaaj*
meat	*l'hem*
vegetables	*legoom/khodra*
water	*maa'a*

Numbers

1	*waa'hid*
2	*zooj*
3	*tlaata*
4	*araba'aa*
5	*khamsa*
6	*set-ta*
7	*seba'a*
8	*tmaanya*
9	*tes'aa*
10	*'ashra*
20	*eshreen*
50	*khamseen*
100	*meya*

ACKNOWLEDGMENTS

This edition updated by

Contributors Sally Kirby, Amanda Mouttaki

Senior Editor Alison McGill

Senior Designers Laura O'Brien, Vinita Venugopal

Project Editors Sarah Allen, Alex Pathe

Project Art Editor Bandana Paul

Editors Abhidha Lakhera, Molly McCarthy

Proofreader Ben Ffrancon Dowds

Indexer Gina Guilinger

Picture Research team Geetam Biswas, Virien Chopra, Nishwan Rasool, Samrajkumar S

Publishing Assistant Simona Velikova

Jacket Designers Laura O'Brien, Vinita Venugopal

Jacket Picture Researcher Claire Guest

Project Cartography Ashif

Senior Cartographer James Macdonald

Cartography Manager Suresh Kumar

Senior DTP Designer Tanveer Zaidi

DTP Designer Rohit Rojal

Pre-production Manager Balwant Singh

Image Retouching-Production Manager Pankaj Sharma

Production Controller Kariss Ainsworth

Managing Editors Beverly Smart, Hollie Teague

Managing Art Editor Gemma Doyle

Senior Managing Art Editor Priyanka Thakur

Art Director Maxine Pedliham

Publishing Director Georgina Dee

DK would like to thank the following for their contribution to the previous editions: Andrew Humphreys, Alan Keohane, Mary Novakovich

The publisher would like to thank the following for their kind permission to reproduce their photographs:

Key: a-above; b-below/bottom; c-center; f-far; l-left; r-right; t-top

123RF.com: Xamnesiacx 12br.

33 rue Majorelle: 84tl.

Alamy Stock Photo: AA World Travel Library 83tl, Abaca Press 46t, Ian Bottle / Carles Arola 81t, Ilyas Ayub 45br, Ian Bottle 72t, Adalgisa Cacciacarne 48bl, Chronicle 8t, Luis Dafos 77bl, Ian Dagnall 65tl, Escapetheofficejob 89bl, Kevin Foy 54tr, FreeProd 62t, Gaertner 104–105t, James Hackland 17b, Hemis / Avenet Pascal 23bl, Hemis / Guiziou Franck 95br, Hemis / Mattes René 11t, 41tr, Hemis / Montico Lionel 13cl (8), 49b, Diane Holmes 29tr, Idealink Photography 55b, imageBROKER.com GmbH & Co. KG / Franz Walter 101br, imageBROKER.com GmbH & Co. KG / Martin Moxter 21br, imageBROKER.com GmbH & Co. KG / Martina Katz 23br, imageBROKER.com GmbH & Co. KG / Wigbert Röth 95t, Imago / Aissa 90b, Impress 10tl, Jam World Images 34bl, Alistair Laming 34clb, 34cb, Y. Levy 34br, Mauritius images GmbH / Andy Ridder 76t, Moroccan vipLens 12cr, Ilpo Musto 59tr, 70bl, Steve Nicholls 63bl, Penta Springs Limited / Artokoloro 9tr, 9br, Photo 12 10br, Olga Popkova 61tr, Prisma Archivo 9bl, Lukasz Puch 98–99t, Robertharding / Jochen Schlenker 102tl, Rowan Romeyn 6–7, Grant Rooney 56t, Kumar Sriskandan 13bl, Petr Svarc 39br, Matthew Taylor 63tr, Tim E White 13clb, 58–59bc, 78tl, Jan Wlodarczyk 50tl, 105br, Andrew Woodley 36bl.

AWL Images: Francesco Riccardo Iacomino 52–53.

David Bloch Art Gallery: David Bloch 13tl.

Depositphotos Inc: Merc67 50–51b, Sabinoparente 19, Saharrr 96–97, Savvatexture 21cr, Wrangel 9cr.

Dreamstime.com: Checco 15bl, Ipek Morel Diplikaya 75tr, Dorinmarius 16tc, 38–39t, 82b, Grantotufo 29tc, Francesco Riccardo Iacomino 37tl, Miroslav Liska 43, Marktucan 20br, Mrsixinthemix 101t, Sergii Velychko 33br.

Dunes & Desert: 57br.

Fondation Jardin Majorelle: Nicolas Mathus 12crb.

Getty Images: 500Px Plus / Vincent Courceleaud 64–65b, AFP 10cl, AFP / Fadel Senna 10bl, Corbis Documentary / Marco Cristofori 20cr, De Agostini / DEA / C. SAPPA 8bl, DigitalVision / Kathrin Ziegler 13cla, 107, DigitalVision / Matteo Colombo 92–93, DigitalVision / Thomas Barwick 5, 14bl, 15cb, Moment / Artur Debat 22t, Moment / Carles Navarro Parcerisas 67, Moment / Chris Griffiths 99br, Moment / Craig Hastings 87tr, Moment / Francesco Riccardo Iacomino 87b, Moment / Photography by Jeremy Villasis. Philippines. 61bl, Moment / Roberto Moiola / Sysaworld 13cl, Stone / Gary Yeowell 60t, Wirelmage / Jason Kempin 47br.

Getty Images / iStock: Balate Dorin 29ca, E+ / Eloi_Omella 69t, E+ / FrankvandenBergh 31t,

- / Pavliha 24–25b, Fabiomichelecapelli
3b, 38bl, Javarman3 45tl, Zdeno_Kajzr 60bl,
elanieMaya 26bl, Olena_Z 32bl, Pavliha 23cb,
Andrey 88t, Starcevic 26–27t, 27br, Wirestock 1.

e Foundouk: 79bl.

aison de la Photographie: 46bl.

Y Kechmara: 85br.

asiria: 56br.

epe Nero: 73br.

iad Noir dIvoire: 48tr.

hutterstock.com: Andocs 12cra, Atosan
0–71tc, Glen Berlin 25tr, Byvalet 32–33t,
adagan 21tc, 35t, Posztos 37b, Edler von
abenstein 29cra, Savvapanf Photo 30bl,
kostep 102–103bc, Todamo 16cl, 40cl, 41b,
9bl, Olena Znak 44b.

aros: 91tr.

over Images:
ront and Spine: **4Corners:** Reinhard Schmid.
ack: **Alamy Stock Photo:** FreeProd tr, Gaertner
; **Getty Images / iStock:** E+ / Pavliha cl.

Sheet Map Cover Images:
Corners: Reinhard Schmid.

All other images © Dorling Kindersley Limited
or further information see: www.dkimages.com

A NOTE FROM DK

The rate at which the world is changing
is constantly keeping the DK travel team
on our toes. While we've worked hard to ensure
that this edition of Marrakech is accurate and
up-to-date, we know that opening hours alter,
standards shift, prices fluctuate, places close
and new ones pop up in their stead. So, if you
notice we've got something wrong or left
something out, we want to hear about it.
Please get in touch at travelguides@dk.com

Within each Top 10 list in this book,
no hierarchy of quality or popularity is
implied. All 10 are, in the editor's opinion,
of roughly equal merit.

First edition 2008

Published in Great Britain by
Dorling Kindersley Limited, DK,
20 Vauxhall Bridge Road, London SW1V 2SA

The authorised representative in the EEA is
Dorling Kindersley Verlag GmbH. Arnulfstr.
124, 80636 Munich, Germany

Published in the United States by DK Publishing,
1745 Broadway, 20th Floor, New York, NY 10019, USA

Copyright © 2008, 2025 Dorling Kindersley Limited
A Penguin Random House Company

24 25 26 27 10 9 8 7 6 5 4 3 2 1

A CIP catalog record for this book
is available from the British Library.

A catalog record for this book is available
from the Library of Congress.

ISSN: 1542 1554
ISBN: 978 0 2416 7707 0

Printed and bound in China

www.dk.com

This book was made with Forest
Stewardship Council™ certified
paper – one small step in DK's
commitment to a sustainable future.
Learn more at **www.dk.com/uk/
information/sustainability**